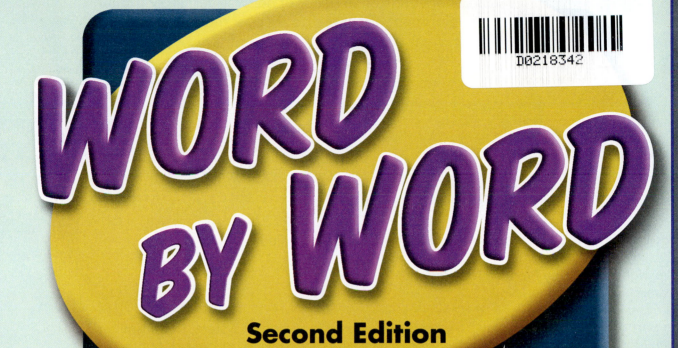

WORD BY WORD

Second Edition

ENGLISH/ KOREAN

영한 그림 사전

Steven J. Molinsky • Bill Bliss

Yang-Sook Shin 번역

삽화
Richard E. Hill

PEARSON
Longman

Dedicated to Janet Johnston in honor of her wonderful contribution to the development of our textbooks over three decades.

Steven J. Molinsky
Bill Bliss

Word by Word Picture Dictionary, English / Korean, second edition

Pearson Education, 10 Bank Street, White Plains, NY 10606

Editorial director: Pam Fishman
Vice president, director of design and production: Rhea Banker
Director of electronic production: Aliza Greenblatt
Director of manufacturing: Patrice Fraccio
Senior manufacturing manager: Edith Pullman
Marketing managers: Kyoko Oinama, Oliva Fernandez
Editorial assistant: Katherine Keyes
Senior digital layout specialist: Wendy Wolf
Text design: Wendy Wolf
Cover design: Tracey Munz Cataldo
Realia creation: Warren Fischbach, Paula Williams
Illustrations: Richard E. Hill
Contributing artists: Steven Young, Charles Cawley, Willard Gage, Marlon Violette
Reviewers: Hyung-Lan Kim, Military Test Prep Lang. Institute, Hannah Park, Guri SPL
Project management by TransPac Education Services, Victoria, BC, Canada
with assistance from Yu Jian Yo, Studio G, & Robert Zacharias

ISBN 0-13-191630-0
Longman on the Web
Longman.com offers online resources for teachers and students. Access our Companion Websites, our online catalog, and our local offices around the world.

Visit us at longman.com.

Printed in the United States of America
6 7 8 9 10 – V042 – 12 11

CONTENTS

목차

WORD BY WORD 그림 사전 2판의 독자 여러분들을 환영합니다.

이 책의 목적은 어휘 학습을 역동적인 커뮤니케이션의 경험으로 생생하게 다가오게 함으로써 학생들이 일상생활과 커뮤니티, 학교, 일터 등에서 성공적으로 영어를 사용할 수 있도록 만드는 일입니다.

편이성과 명확성을 고려하여 분명하고도 생동감 있는 삽화들과 간편한 학습 페이지들이 모든 레벨의 학습자들을 위해 만들어졌습니다.

세심한 연구를 바탕으로 짠 교과 배열을 통하여 4,000개 이상의 어휘들과 138개 토픽들을 제공함으로써 학생들이 문법과 어휘 실력을 통합적으로 키울 수 있게 하였습니다.

모범 대화는 사람들이 실제 대화에서 단어들을 사용하는 배경들과 상황들을 묘사해줍니다. 학생들은 이러한 모범 대화들을 바탕으로 각 과에서 그 단어들을 사용해 새로운 대화를 만들면서 다이내믹한 쌍방향 대화 훈련에 참여하게 됩니다.

거실

책장	1	bookcase	벽	10	wall	소파	20	sofa/couch
사진	2	picture/photograph	천장	11	ceiling	화초	21	plant
그림	3	painting	커튼	12	drapes	응접실 탁자	22	coffee table
벽난로 선반	4	mantel	창문	13	window	융단	23	rug
벽난로	5	fireplace	2인용 소파	14	loveseat	램프	24	lamp
벽난로 가리개	6	fireplace screen	벽 장식장	15	wall unit	램프 갓	25	lampshade
벽난로 스크린			스피커	16	speaker	구석 테이블	26	end table
DVD 재생기	7	DVD player	스테레오 시스템	17	stereo system	마루	27	floor
텔레비전	8	television/TV	잡지 보관함	18	magazine holder	마루 전기 스텐드	28	floor lamp
비디오 카세트	9	VCR/video	(장식용)쿠션,베개	19	(throw) pillow	안락의자	29	armchair
녹화기		cassette recorder						

A. Where are you?
B. I'm in the living room.
A. What are you doing?
B. I'm dusting* the **bookcase**.

* dusting/cleaning

A. You have a very nice living room!
B. Thank you.
A. Your _____ is/are beautiful!
B. Thank you for saying so.

A. Uh-oh! I just spilled coffee on your _____!
B. That's okay. Don't worry about it.

Tell about your living room.
(In my living room there's ....)

추가 대화들을 통하여 학생들은 좀 더 연장된 상황에서 어휘를 사용해 볼 수 있으며, 칭찬, 사과 또는 정보의 요청 등과 같이 주요한 기능적 커뮤니케이션 기술을 익힐 수 있게 됩니다.

각 과에서 작문과 토론용 질문들을 통하여 학생들이 자기 자신과 자기 문화 그리고 자신들의 국가에 대한 경험과 생각, 의견, 정보 등을 함께 나눔으로써 그 어휘들과 주제들을 자신들의 실제 생활과 연관시키도록 합니다.

수업 전략

이 교사 지침서는 *Word by Word*의 각 과에 대한 단계별 지침들을 제공하고 있습니다. 각 과에서 어휘들을 보여주고 익히도록 하기 위해 제시된 전략들을 여기에서 잠깐 살펴 보겠습니다.

1 ▶ **어휘를 미리 보여줍니다:** 학생들이 이미 알고 있는 단어들을 브레인스토밍을 하며 칠판에 쓰거나 혹은 *Word by Word*의 그림이나 슬라이드를 보게 하여 친숙한 단어들을 상기시켜 학생들의 기존의 지식들을 활성화시키십시오.

2 ▶ **어휘를 제시합니다:** 그림 사전에 있는 그림이나 슬라이드를 사용하여 각 단어들을 집거나, 말하거나 교실 전체가 한꺼번에 혹은 개개인별로 반복하게 합니다. (오디오 프로그램으로 단어 리스트를 들려줄 수도 있습니다.) 어휘에 대한 학생들의 이해와 발음을 확인합니다.

3 ▶ **어휘 훈련:** 학생들에게 단어를 교실 전체가 한꺼번에, 혹은 짝을 짓거나 작은 그룹별로 연습하게 합니다. 단어를 말하거나 쓰고 학생들에게 그 물건을 가리키게 하거나 번호를 말하게 합니다. 혹은 어떤 물건을 가리키거나 번호를 주고 학생들에게 그 단어를 말하게 합니다.

4 ▶ **모범 대화 훈련:** 어떤 과들에서는 모범 대화들이 어휘 리스트의 첫 번째 단어를 사용하고 있습니다. 다른 모범 대화들은 단어들을 삽입할 수 있는 괄호가 있는 골격 대화 문장으로 이루어져 있습니다.

- a. 미리 보기: 학생들에게 모델 그림을 보여주고 말하는 사람이 누구인지 어느 장소에서 대화가 이루어지고 있는지에 대해 토론하도록 합니다.
- b. 교사가 모범 대화를 제시하고 오디오를 한번 이상 들려준 다음 학생들이 어휘와 상황에 대해 잘 이해하고 있는지 확인합니다.
- c. 대화의 각 문장을 학생 전체가 다 함께 또는 개별적으로 반복합니다.
- d. 학생들이 짝을 지어 모범 대화를 연습합니다.
- e. 학생들이 짝과 함께 어휘 리스트에서 다른 단어를 사용하여 모범 대화를 바탕으로 한 대화를 만들어 제시합니다.
- f. 학생들이 짝끼리 그 페이지에 있는 다른 단어들을 사용하여 모범 대화를 바탕으로 한 여러 대화를 연습합니다.
- g. 짝들이 나와 연습한 대화를 전체 학생들에게 보여 주게 합니다.

5 ▶ **추가 대화 훈련:** 많은 과들은 어휘를 좀더 대화식으로 연습할 수 있도록 두 개의 추가 골격 대화문을 제공하고 있습니다. 학생들에게 원하는 단어를 사용해 이 대화문들을 연습하고 발표하도록 합니다. 추가 대화문을 연습하기 전에 학생들에게 오디오 프로그램의 추가 대화문을 샘플로 들려줄 수 있습니다.

6 ▶ **스펠링 훈련:** 학생들에게 전체적으로나 짝을 짓거나 혹은 소그룹으로 단어 스펠링을 연습하게 합니다. 어떤 단어를 말하고 학생들에게 그 스펠링을 크게 말하게 하거나 적도록 합니다. 혹은 슬라이드를 이용해 어느 물건을 가리키고 학생들에게 그 단어를 적도록 합니다.

7 ▶ **토론, 작문, 일기, 포트폴리오를 위한 주제:** 학생들에게 반 전체나 혹은 짝을 짓거나 소그룹으로 (페이지 하단에 있는) 질문에 대답하도록 합니다. 혹은 학생들에게 집에서 답을 적어와 다른 학생들과 함께 공유하며, 반 전체나 혹은 짝을 짓거나 소그룹으로 토론하게 합니다. 학생들이 자신의 작문들을 일지 형식으로 보관할 수 있습니다. 이 작문들은 학생 자신들의 작업 포트폴리오로서 자신들의 실력 향상을 보여주는 실제 예가 됩니다.

8 ▶ **연장 활동:** 교사 지침서는 학생들의 어휘 학습을 강화시키고 확대시키기 위해 아주 다양한 자료들을 제공합니다.

Word by Word 그림 사전 2판의 독자 여러분들을 환영합니다. 이 책은 생생한 삽화들과 모든 레벨의 학습자들을 위해 편이성과 명확성을 고려하여 만들어진 간편한 교과 페이지들을 통하여 4000여 단어의 어휘를 제공하고 있습니다. 이 책의 목적은 학생들이 일상 생활과 커뮤니티, 학교, 일터 또는 해외 여행 등에서 사용되는 영어를 연습할 수 있도록 돕는 것입니다.

WORD BY WORD 는 어휘들을 17개 주제 단원으로 나누어 실었으며 세심한 연구를 바탕으로 짠 교과 일정을 제공하여 바로 자기 주변 세계부터 시작하여 바깥 모든 세계에 이르는 토픽들을 통해 학생들이 문법 향상과 어휘 실력을 통합적으로 키울 수 있도록 하였습니다. 가족, 가정, 일상 활동에 대한 교과로부터 시작하여 지역 사회, 학교, 일터, 쇼핑, 레크레이션 및 기타 토픽들로 이어집니다. 학생들의 어휘를 발전시키는 것과 더불어 이 교재는 또한 전반적인 커뮤니케이션 기술 프로그램으로서 어휘 학습, 리스닝 및 스피킹 기술 그리고 작문과 토론을 위한 주제 등을 통합적으로 다루고 있습니다. 이전 페이지에 실린 The Scope & Sequence 는 이 프로그램의 독특한 커리큘럼과 기술 통합(skill integration) 을 잘 보여주고 있습니다.

Word by Word 의 모든 과는 독립적으로 구성되어서 순차적으로든 학습자가 원하는 순서대로든 사용할 수 있습니다. 학습자들의 편의를 위하여 각 과는 두 가지 방식으로 목록이 만들어졌습니다. 목차에서는 내용 순서대로 정리되었고 주제별 인덱스에서는 알파벳 순으로 되었습니다. 이 자료들은 부록의 용어집(Glossary) 과 더불어서 학생들이나 교사들이 빠르고 쉽게 이 그림 사전의 모든 단어들과 토픽들을 찾을 수 있게 해줍니다.

모든 레벨의 교육을 위해 좀더 폭 넓게 선별된 인쇄 및 미디어 자료선(資料選)인 Word by Word Vocabulary Development Program 중, 이 Word by Word Picture Dictionary 가 핵심적인 요체입니다.

다른 레벨들의 각 워크북들은 학생들의 필요에 맞게 유통성 있는 옵션을 제공하고 있습니다. 초급과 중급 레벨의 어휘 워크북들은 어휘, 문법 그리고 리스닝 연습 등에 중점을 두고 있습니다. Literacy 워크북은 특별히 알파벳에 익숙하지 않은 학습자들이나 또는 영어 어휘, 읽기, 쓰기 등에 대해서 초급 이전 단계의 설명이 필요한 학생들을

위해 전반적 기술 연습(all-skills practice)을 할 수 있도록 하고 있습니다.

CD-Rom 이 있는 교사 지침서와 레슨 프랜너에는 레슨 프래닝에 대한 제안, 커뮤니티 태스크, 인터넷 웹 링크 그리고 선생님들의 수업 준비 시간을 절약해 줄 수 있는 복사 가능 원본 자료(reproducible masters)등이 포함되어 있습니다. 주요 어휘 향상 활동을 위한 단계별 교육 전략을 담은 Activity Handbook 도 교사 지침서에 포함되어 있습니다.

오디오 프로그램에는 모든 단어들 및 쌍방향 대화 훈련을 위한 회화 등이 들어 있으며, 보너스 자료로서 어휘를 가지고 뮤지컬로 즐겁게 연습할 수 있는 워드 송(WordSong)들도 선별적으로 실리었습니다.

추가로 부수적인 자료로서 칼라 슬라이드 필름, 어휘 게임 카드, 테스트 프로그램, 그리고 ExamView CD-ROM 이 실려 있습니다.

수업 전략

Word by Word 는 문맥 상에서의 어휘들을 제시해줍니다. 모범 대화들은 사람들이 실제 대화에서 그 단어를 사용하는 상황들을 묘사해줍니다. 이러한 모범 대화들을 기본으로 하여 학생들은 다이내믹한 쌍방향 대화 훈련에 참여하게 됩니다. 또한 각 과에 있는 작문과 토론용 질문을 통하여 학생들이 자신들의 국가와 문화 혹은 자신에 대한 경험과 생각, 의견, 정보 등을 공유함으로써 그 어휘들과 주제들을 그들의 실제 생활과 연관시키도록 합니다. 이런식으로 학생들은 "word by word" 를 통해서 서로를 알게 됩니다.

Word by Word 를 사용함으로써 우리는 여러분들의 교수 스타일 뿐만 아니라 학생들의 능력과 필요에 맞는 방식과 전략을 개발하도록 도와줍니다. 어휘 제시와 연습을 위

해서 다음과 같은 테크닉을 함께 사용하는 것이 도움이 될 것입니다.

1. **어휘를 미리 보여줍니다:** 학생들이 이미 알고 있는 단어들을 브레인스토밍을 하며 칠판에 쓰거나 혹은 Word by Word의 그림이나 슬라이드를 보게 하여 친숙한 단어들을 상기시키며 학생들의 기존의 지식들을 활성화시키십시오.

2. **어휘를 제시합니다:** 그림 사전에 있는 그림이나 슬라이드를 사용하여 각 단어들을 집거나, 말하거나 교실 전체가 한꺼번에 혹은 개개인별로 반복하게 합니다. (오디오 프로그램으로 단어 리스트를 들려줄 수도 있습니다.) 어휘에 대한 학생들의 이해와 발음을 확인합니다.

3. **어휘 훈련:** 학생들에게 단어를 교실 전체가 한꺼번에, 혹은 짝을 짓거나 작은 그룹별로 연습하게 합니다. 단어를 말하거나 써서 학생들에게 그 물건을 가리키게 하거나 번호를 말하게 합니다. 혹은 어떤 물건을 가리키거나 번호를 주고 학생들에게 그 단어를 말하게 합니다.

4. **모범 대화 훈련:** 어떤 교과들에서는 어휘 리스트의 첫번째 단어를 사용하는 모범 대화가 있습니다. 다른 모범 대화들은 단어들을 삽입할 수 있는 괄호가 있는 골격 대화 문장으로 이루어져 있습니다. (많은 경우 골격 문장에서 괄호 안의 숫자는 그 대화를 연습할 때 사용될 수 있는 단어를 가리킵니다. 괄호 안의 숫자가 표시 되어 있지 않은 경우는 그 과의 모든 단어가 사용될 수 있습니다.)

다음과 같은 단계로 모범 대화 훈련을 하기를 권장합니다:

a. 미리 보기: 학생들에게 모델 그림을 보여주고 말하는 사람이 누구인지 어느 장소에서 대화가 이루어지고 있는지에 대해 토론하도록 합니다.

b. 교사가 모범 대화를 제시하고 오디오를 한번 이상 들려준 다음 학생들이 어휘와 상황에 대해 잘 이해하고 있는지 확인합니다.

c. 대화의 각 문장을 학생 전체가 다 함께 또는 개별적으로 반복합니다.

d. 학생들이 짝을 지어 모범 대화를 연습합니다.

e. 학생들이 짝과 함께 어휘 리스트에서 다른 단어를 사용하여 모범 대화를 바탕으로 한 대화를 만들어 제시합니다.

f. 학생들이 짝끼리 그 페이지에 있는 다른 단어들을 사용하여 모범 대화를 바탕으로 한 여러 대화를 연습합니다.

g. 짝들이 나와 연습한 대화를 전체 학생들에게 보여주게 합니다.

5. **추가 대화 훈련:** 많은 과들은 어휘를 좀더 대화식으로 연습할 수 있도록 두 개의 추가 골격 대화문을 제공하고 있습니다. (페이지 하단에 옅은 노란색 부분에 나타나 있습니다.) 학생들에게 원하는 단어를 사용해 이 대화문들을 연습하고 발표하도록 합니다. 추가 대화문을 연습하기 전에 학생들에게 오디오 프로그램의 추가 대화문을 샘플로 들려줄 수 있습니다.

6. **스펠링 훈련:** 학생들에게 전체적으로나 짝을 짓거나 혹은 소그룹으로 단어 스펠링을 연습하게 합니다. 어떤 단어를 말하고 학생들에게 그 스펠링을 크게 말하게 하거나 적도록 합니다. 혹은 슬라이드를 이용해 어느 물건을 가리키고 학생들에게 그 단어를 적도록 합니다.

7. **토론, 작문, 일기, 포트폴리오를 위한 주제:** *Word by Word*의 모든 교과는 하나 이상의 토론 및 작문을 위한 질문을 줍니다. (페이지 하단의 옅은 파란색 부분에 나타나 있습니다.) 학생들에게 반 전체나 짝을 짓거나 혹은 소그룹으로 질문에 대답하도록 합니다. 혹은 학생들에게 집에서 답을 적어와 다른 학생들과 함께 공유하며, 반 전체나 짝을 짓거나 소그룹으로 토론하게 합니다.

학생들이 일지 식으로 작문하는 것을 좋아할 수 있습니다. 시간이 허락되면 교사가 각 학생들의 작문에 자신의 견해와 경험 등을 첨언하여 학생들이 작문한 것에 대해 의견을 줄 수도 있습니다. 학생들의 작품을 포트폴리오로 보관하게 되면, 이 작문들은 학생들의 영어 실력 향상의 훌륭한 본보기가 됩니다.

8. **커뮤니케이션 활동:** CD-ROM이 딸린 *Word by Word* 교사 가이드와 레슨 프래너 (Lesson Planner) 는 학생들 나름의 색다른 학습 스타일과 특정한 능력이나 강점들을 활용할 수 있도록 고안된 각종 게임들과 과제, 브레인스토밍, 토론, 움직임, 그리기, 마임, 역할 놀이 등과 그 밖의 활동들을 제공합니다. 매 과마다, 자극적이고 창조적이고 재미 있는 방식으로 학생들이 어휘 학습을 강화할 수 있도록 하나 이상의 활동들을 선택하십시오.

WORD BY WORD 는 실질적이고도 생생한 대화식 영어 단어 학습 방법을 학생들에게 주고자 합니다. 여러분들에게 이 프로그램의 요지를 얘기하면서, 동시에 우리는 단어 학습이 실제로 쌍방향일 수 있으며...학생들의 생활과 연관될 수 있으며... 학생들 나름의 강점들과 학습 스타일에 따라 달라질 수 있으며... 그리고 재미 있을 수 있는 일이라는 우리의 뜻까지도 알리고 싶습니다.

Steven J. Molinsky
Bill Bliss

Welcome to the second edition of the *WORD BY WORD* Picture Dictionary! This text presents more than 4,000 vocabulary words through vibrant illustrations and simple accessible lesson pages that are designed for clarity and ease-of-use with learners at all levels. Our goal is to help students practice English used in everyday life, in the community, in school, at work, and in international travel.

WORD BY WORD organizes the vocabulary into 17 thematic units, providing a careful research-based sequence of lessons that integrates students' development of grammar and vocabulary skills through topics that begin with the immediate world of the student and progress to the world at large. Early lessons on the family, the home, and daily activities lead to lessons on the community, school, workplace, shopping, recreation, and other topics. In addition to developing students' vocabulary, the text also serves as a comprehensive communication skills program that integrates vocabulary learning, listening and speaking skills, and themes for writing and discussion.

Since each lesson in *Word by Word* is self-contained, it can be used either sequentially or in any desired order. For users' convenience, the lessons are listed in two ways: sequentially in the Table of Contents, and alphabetically in the Thematic Index. These resources, combined with the Glossary in the appendix, allow students and teachers to quickly and easily locate all words and topics in the Picture Dictionary.

The *Word by Word* Picture Dictionary is the centerpiece of the complete *Word by Word* Vocabulary Development Program, which offers a wide selection of print and media support materials for instruction at all levels.

Workbooks at different levels offer flexible options to meet students' needs. Vocabulary Workbooks at Beginning and Intermediate levels feature motivating vocabulary, grammar, and listening practice. A Literacy Workbook provides all-skills practice especially appropriate for learners who are not familiar with the alphabet or who need a pre-Beginning-level introduction to English vocabulary, reading, and writing.

The Teacher's Guide and Lesson Planner with CD-ROM includes lesson-planning suggestions, community tasks, Internet weblinks, and reproducible masters to save teachers hours of lesson preparation time. An Activity Handbook with step-by-step teaching strategies for key vocabulary development activities is included in the Teacher's Guide.

The Audio Program includes all words and conversations for interactive practice and —as bonus material—an expanded selection of WordSongs for entertaining musical practice with the vocabulary.

Additional ancillary materials include Color Transparencies, Vocabulary Game Cards, a Testing Program, and ExamView CD-ROM. Bilingual Editions are also available.

Teaching Strategies

Word by Word presents vocabulary words in context. Model conversations depict situations in which people use the words in meaningful communication. These models become the basis for students to engage in dynamic, interactive practice. In addition, writing and discussion questions in each lesson encourage students to relate the vocabulary and themes to their own lives as they share experiences, thoughts, opinions, and information about themselves, their cultures, and their countries. In this way, students get to know each other "word by word."

In using *Word by Word*, we encourage you to develop approaches and strategies that are compatible with your own teaching style and the needs and abilities of your students. You may find it helpful to incorporate some of the following techniques for presenting and practicing the vocabulary in each lesson.

1. **Preview the Vocabulary:** Activate students' prior knowledge of the vocabulary by brainstorming with students the words in the lesson they already know and writing them on the board, or by having students look at the transparency or the illustration in *Word by Word* and identify the words they are familiar with.

2. **Present the Vocabulary:** Using the transparency or the illustration in the Picture Dictionary, point to the picture of each word, say the word, and have the class repeat it chorally and individually. (You can also play the word list on the Audio Program.) Check students' understanding and pronunciation of the vocabulary.

3. **Vocabulary Practice:** Have students practice the vocabulary as a class, in pairs, or in small groups. Say or write a word, and have students point to the item or tell the number. Or, point to an item or give the number, and have students say the word.

4. **Model Conversation Practice:** Some lessons have model conversations that use the first word in the vocabulary list. Other models are in the form of skeletal dialogs, in which vocabulary words can be inserted. (In many skeletal dialogs, bracketed numbers indicate which words can be used for practicing the conversation. If no bracketed numbers appear, all the words in the lesson can be used.)

The following steps are recommended for Model Conversation Practice:

   a. Preview: Have students look at the model illustration and discuss who they think the speakers are and where the conversation takes place.

   b. The teacher presents the model or plays the audio one or more times and checks students' understanding of the situation and the vocabulary.

   c. Students repeat each line of the conversation chorally and individually.

   d. Students practice the model in pairs.

   e. A pair of students presents a conversation based on the model, but using a different word from the vocabulary list.

   f. In pairs, students practice several conversations based on the model, using different words on the page.

   g. Pairs present their conversations to the class.

5. **Additional Conversation Practice:** Many lessons provide two additional skeletal dialogs for further conversation practice with the vocabulary. (These can be found in the yellow-shaded area at the bottom of the page.) Have students practice and present these conversations using any words they wish. Before they practice the additional conversations, you may want to have students listen to the sample additional conversations on the Audio Program.

6. **Spelling Practice:** Have students practice spelling the words as a class, in pairs, or in small groups. Say a word, and have students spell it aloud or write it. Or, using the transparency, point to an item and have students write the word.

7. **Themes for Discussion, Composition, Journals, and Portfolios:** Each lesson of *Word by Word* provides one or more questions for discussion and composition. (These can be found in a blue-shaded area at the bottom of the page.) Have students respond to the questions as a class, in pairs, or in small groups. Or, have students write their responses at home, share their written work with other students, and discuss as a class, in pairs, or in small groups.

Students may enjoy keeping a journal of their written work. If time permits, you may want to write a response in each student's journal, sharing your own opinions and experiences as well as reacting to what the student has written. If you are keeping portfolios of students' work, these compositions serve as excellent examples of students' progress in learning English.

8. **Communication Activities:** The *Word by Word* Teacher's Guide and Lesson Planner with CD-ROM provides a wealth of games, tasks, brainstorming, discussion, movement, drawing, miming, role-playing, and other activities designed to take advantage of students' different learning styles and particular abilities and strengths. For each lesson, choose one or more of these activities to reinforce students' vocabulary learning in a way that is stimulating, creative, and enjoyable.

WORD BY WORD aims to offer students a communicative, meaningful, and lively way of practicing English vocabulary. In conveying to you the substance of our program, we hope that we have also conveyed the spirit: that learning vocabulary can be genuinely interactive . . . relevant to our students' lives . . . responsive to students' differing strengths and learning styles . . . and fun!

Steven J. Molinsky

Bill Bliss

개인 정보

Registration Form

Name	Gloria	P.	Sánchez
	First	Middle Initial	Last

Address	95	Garden Street	3G
	Number	Street	Apartment Number
	Los Angeles	CA	90036
	City	State	Zip Code

Telephone ___323-524-3278___   Cell Phone ___323-695-1864___

E-Mail Address ___gloria97@ail.com___   SSN ___227-93-6185___   Sex M__ F **X**

Date of Birth ___5/12/88___   Place of Birth ___Centerville, Texas___

이름	**1** name	우편번호	**11** zip code
이름	**2** first name	지역번호	**12** area code
중간 이름 첫글자	**3** middle initial	전화번호	**13** telephone number/ phone number
성	**4** last name/family name/ surname	휴대폰 번호	**14** cell phone number
주소	**5** address	이메일 주소	**15** e-mail address
번지/거리번호	**6** street number	사회보장번호/주민등록 번호	**16** social security number
거리	**7** street	성별	**17** sex
아파트 번호	**8** apartment number	생일	**18** date of birth
도시	**9** city	출생지	**19** place of birth
주	**10** state		

A. What's your **name**?
B. Gloria P. Sánchez.

A. What's your _____?
B. ....
A. Did you say ....?
B. Yes. That's right.

A. What's your last name?
B. ....
A. How do you spell that?
B. ....

Tell about yourself:
    My name is ....
    My address is ....
    My telephone number is ....

Now interview a friend.

가족구성원 I

남편	**1** husband		자녀	**children**		조부모	**grandparents**
아내	**2** wife		딸	**5** daughter		할머니	**10** grandmother
			아들	**6** son		할아버지	**11** grandfather
부모	**parents**		아기	**7** baby			
아버지	**3** father					손주	**grandchildren**
어머니	**4** mother		형제 자매	**siblings**		손녀	**12** granddaughter
			여자 형제/언니/누나/여동생	**8** sister		손자	**13** grandson
			남자형제/오빠/형/남동생	**9** brother			

A. Who is he?
B. He's my **husband**.
A. What's his name?
B. His name is *Jack*.

A. Who is she?
B. She's my **wife**.
A. What's her name?
B. Her name is *Nancy*.

A. I'd like to introduce my _____.
B. Nice to meet you.
C. Nice to meet you, too.

A. What's your _____'s name?
B. His/Her name is ....

Who are the people in your family?
What are their names?

Tell about photos of family members.

Helen   Walter

Jack   Nancy   Frank   Linda

Jennifer   Timmy   Alan

(외)삼촌/백부/숙부/ 고모부/이모부	**1**	uncle
백모/숙모/고모/이모	**2**	aunt
조카딸	**3**	niece
조카	**4**	nephew
사촌	**5**	cousin

장모/시어머니	**6**	mother-in-law
장인/시아버지	**7**	father-in-law
사위	**8**	son-in-law
며느리	**9**	daughter-in-law
매부/매형/시동생/아주버니/처남	**10**	brother-in-law
동서/시누이/형수/처제/처형	**11**	sister-in-law

① Jack is Alan's ___.
② Nancy is Alan's ___.
③ Jennifer is Frank and Linda's ___.
④ Timmy is Frank and Linda's ___.
⑤ Alan is Jennifer and Timmy's ___.

⑥ Helen is Jack's ___.
⑦ Walter is Jack's ___.
⑧ Jack is Helen and Walter's ___.
⑨ Linda is Helen and Walter's ___.
⑩ Frank is Jack's ___.
⑪ Linda is Jack's ___.

A. Who is he/she?
B. He's/She's my _____.
A. What's his/her name?
B. His/Her name is _____.

A. Let me introduce my _____.
B. I'm glad to meet you.
C. Nice meeting you, too.

Tell about your relatives:
What are their names?
Where do they live?

Draw your family tree and tell about it.

교실

교사/선생님	**1**	teacher	오버헤드 프로젝터	**8**	overhead projector	화이트 보드/	**15**	whiteboard/
보조교사	**2**	teacher's aide	스크린	**9**	screen	칠판		board
학생	**3**	student	칠판/판	**10**	chalkboard/board	지구본	**16**	globe
책상	**4**	desk	시계	**11**	clock	책꽂이/	**17**	bookcase/
좌석/의자	**5**	seat/chair	지도	**12**	map	책장		bookshelf
탁자	**6**	table	게시판	**13**	bulletin board	교사용 책상	**18**	teacher's desk
컴퓨터	**7**	computer	확성기/스피커	**14**	P.A. system/ loudspeaker	쓰레기통	**19**	wastebasket

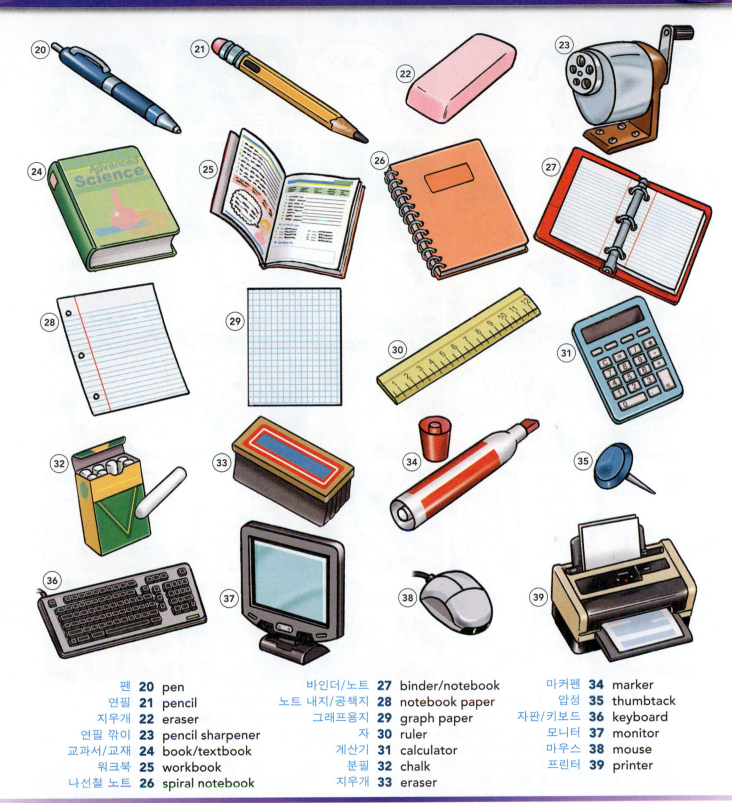

펜	**20**	pen
연필	**21**	pencil
지우개	**22**	eraser
연필 깎이	**23**	pencil sharpener
교과서/교재	**24**	book/textbook
워크북	**25**	workbook
나선철 노트	**26**	spiral notebook
바인더/노트	**27**	binder/notebook
노트 내지/공책지	**28**	notebook paper
그래프용지	**29**	graph paper
자	**30**	ruler
계산기	**31**	calculator
분필	**32**	chalk
지우개	**33**	eraser
마커펜	**34**	marker
압정	**35**	thumbtack
자판/키보드	**36**	keyboard
모니터	**37**	monitor
마우스	**38**	mouse
프린터	**39**	printer

A. Where's the **teacher**?
B. The **teacher** is *next to* the **board**.

A. Where's the **globe**?
B. The **globe** is *on* the **bookcase**.

A. Is there a/an _____ in your classroom?*
B. Yes. There's a/an _____
next to/on the _____.

A. Is there a/an _____ in your classroom?*
B. No, there isn't.

Describe your classroom.
(There's a/an ....)

* With 28, 29, 32 use: Is there _____ in your classroom?

교실내 활동

이름을 말하세요.	**1** Say your name.	손을 드세요.	**16** Raise your hand.
이름을 다시 말하세요.	**2** Repeat your name.	질문하세요.	**17** Ask a question.
이름의 철자를 말하세요.	**3** Spell your name.	질문을 들으세요.	**18** Listen to the question.
이름을 쓰세요.	**4** Print your name.	질문에 답하세요.	**19** Answer the question.
서명하세요.	**5** Sign your name.	답을 들으세요.	**20** Listen to the answer.
일어나세요.	**6** Stand up.	숙제를 하세요.	**21** Do your homework.
칠판으로 가세요.	**7** Go to the board.	숙제를 가져오세요.	**22** Bring in your homework.
칠판에 쓰세요.	**8** Write on the board.	답안을 검토하세요.	**23** Go over the answers.
칠판을 지우세요.	**9** Erase the board.	틀린 답을 정정하세요.	**24** Correct your mistakes.
자리에 앉으세요.	**10** Sit down./Take your seat.	숙제를 제출하세요.	**25** Hand in your homework.
책을 펴세요.	**11** Open your book.	책을 같이 보세요.	**26** Share a book.
10페이지를 읽으세요.	**12** Read page ten.	문제에 대해 토의하세요.	**27** Discuss the question.
10페이지를 공부하세요.	**13** Study page ten.	서로 도우세요.	**28** Help each other.
책을 덮으세요.	**14** Close your book.	함께 공부하세요.	**29** Work together.
책을 치우세요.	**15** Put away your book.	반 학생들에게 발표하세요.	**30** Share with the class.

사전을 찾으세요.	31	Look in the dictionary.
단어를 찾으세요.	32	Look up a word.
단어를 발음하세요.	33	Pronounce the word.
뜻을 읽으세요.	34	Read the definition.
단어를 베끼세요.	35	Copy the word.
자습하세요.	36	Work alone./ Do your own work.
짝과 공부하세요.	37	Work with a partner.
소그룹으로 나누세요.	38	Break up into small groups.
그룹으로 공부하세요.	39	Work in a group.
반 전체가 같이 공부하세요.	40	Work as a class.
커튼을 내리세요.	41	Lower the shades.
전등을 끄세요.	42	Turn off the lights.
스크린을 보세요.	43	Look at the screen.
기록하세요.	44	Take notes.
전등을 켜세요.	45	Turn on the lights.
종이 한장을 꺼내세요.	46	Take out a piece of paper.
시험지를 돌리세요.	47	Pass out the tests.
질문에 답하세요.	48	Answer the questions.
답안을 확인하세요.	49	Check your answers.
시험지를 걷으세요.	50	Collect the tests.
정답을 고르세요.	51	Choose the correct answer.
정답에 동그라미하세요.	52	Circle the correct answer.
빈칸을 채우세요.	53	Fill in the blank.
답에 검은 원을 채워 표시하세요.	54	Mark the answer sheet./ Bubble the answer.
단어를 짝 맞추어 연결하세요.	55	Match the words.
단어에 밑줄을 치세요.	56	Underline the word.
단어를 줄을 그어 지우세요.	57	Cross out the word.
단어의 철자를 정렬하세요.	58	Unscramble the word.
단어를 순서대로 정렬하세요.	59	Put the words in order.
다른 종이에 쓰세요.	60	Write on a separate sheet of paper.

You're the teacher! Give instructions to your students!

전치사

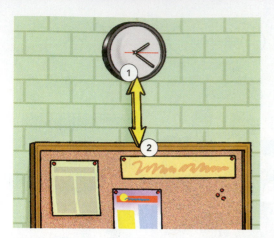

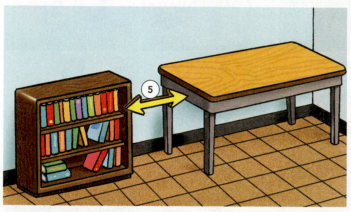

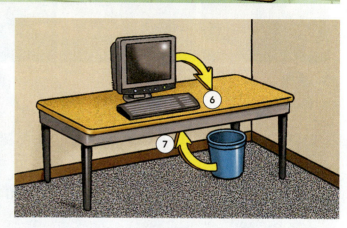

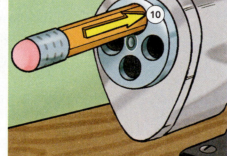

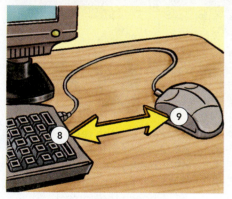

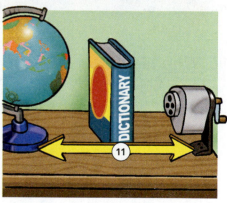

~ 위에	**1** above	~ 위에	**6** on	~ 안에	**10** in
~ 아래	**2** below	~ 밑에	**7** under	~ 사이에	**11** between
~ 앞에	**3** in front of	~ 의 왼쪽으로	**8** to the left of		
~ 뒤에	**4** behind	~ 의 오른쪽으로	**9** to the right of		
~ 옆에	**5** next to				

[1–10]
A. Where's the *clock*?
B. The *clock* is **above** the *bulletin board*.

[11]
A. Where's the *dictionary*?
B. The *dictionary* is **between** the *globe* and the *pencil sharpener*.

Tell about the classroom on page 4. Use the prepositions in this lesson.   Tell about your classroom.

매일 일상 활동 I

일어나다	**1** get up	옷을 벗다	**11** get undressed
샤워하다	**2** take a shower	목욕하다	**12** take a bath
이를 닦다	**3** brush *my** teeth	잠자리에 들다	**13** go to bed
면도하다	**4** shave	잠자다	**14** sleep
옷을 입다	**5** get dressed	아침식사를 준비하다	**15** make breakfast
세수하다	**6** wash *my** face	점심식사를 준비하다	**16** make lunch
화장하다	**7** put on makeup	저녁식사를 요리하다	**17** cook / make dinner
브러쉬로 머리를 빗다	**8** brush *my** hair	아침을 먹다	**18** eat / have breakfast
머리를 빗다	**9** comb *my** hair	점심을 먹다	**19** eat / have lunch
잠자리를 정돈하다	**10** make the bed	저녁을 먹다	**20** eat / have dinner

* my, his, her, our, your, their

A. What do you do every day?
B. I **get up**, I **take a shower**, and I **brush my teeth**.

A. What does he do every day?
B. He _____s, he _____s,
   and he _____s.

A. What does she do every day?
B. She _____s, she _____s,
   and she_____s.

What do you do every day? Make a list.

Interview some friends and tell about their everyday activities.

매일 일상 활동 II

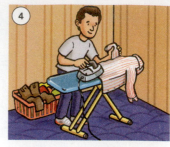

아파트를 청소하다	**1**	clean the apartment/ clean the house
설거지하다	**2**	wash the dishes
세탁하다/빨래하다	**3**	do the laundry
다림질하다	**4**	iron
아기에게 음식을 먹이다	**5**	feed the baby
고양이에게 먹이를 주다	**6**	feed the cat
개를 산책시키다	**7**	walk the dog
공부하다	**8**	study

출근하다	**9**	go to work
학교에 가다	**10**	go to school
자동차로 출근하다	**11**	drive to work
통학 버스를 타다	**12**	take the bus to school
일하다	**13**	work
퇴근하다	**14**	leave work
가게에 가다	**15**	go to the store
집으로 돌아오다	**16**	come home/get home

A. Hello. What are you doing?
B. I'm **clean**ing the **apartment**.

A. Hello, ... This is .... What are you doing?
B. I'm _____ing. How about you?
A. I'm _____ing.

A. Are you going to _____ soon?
B. Yes. I'm going to _____ in a little while.

What are you going to do tomorrow? Make a list of everything you are going to do.

여가 활동들

텔레비전을 보다	1	watch TV	기타를 치다	9	play the guitar
라디오를 듣다	2	listen to the radio	피아노 연습을 하다	10	practice the piano
음악을 듣다	3	listen to music	운동하다	11	exercise
책을 읽다	4	read a book	수영하다	12	swim
신문을 읽다	5	read the newspaper	꽃을 심다	13	plant flowers
놀다	6	play	컴퓨터를 사용하다	14	use the computer
카드 놀이를 하다	7	play cards	편지를 쓰다	15	write a letter
농구하다	8	play basketball	쉬다	16	relax

A. Hi. What are you doing?
B. I'm **watch**ing **TV.**

A. Hi, ... Are you _____ing?
B. No, I'm not. I'm _____ing.

A. What's your (husband/wife/son/daughter/. . .) doing?
B. He's/She's _____ing.

What leisure activities do you like to do?

What do your family members and friends like to do?

Greeting People 인사하기

Leave Taking 작별

안녕하세요.	**1**	Hello. / Hi.	무슨 새로운/별다른 일이라도 있나요?/	**7** What's new?/ What's new with you?
안녕하십니까? (아침에).	**2**	Good morning.	어떻게 지내나요?	
안녕하십니까? (오후에).	**3**	Good afternoon.	별일 없어요/별다른 일 없어요.	**8** Not much. / Not too much.
안녕하십니까? (저녁에).	**4**	Good evening.	안녕히 지내세요!	**9** Good-bye. / Bye.
잘 지내시고 계십니까?	**5**	How are you?/ How are you doing?	안녕히 주무세요.	**10** Good night.
잘 지냅니다.	**6**	Fine. / Fine, thanks. / Okay.	나중에 봐요.	**11** See you later. / See you soon.

Introducing Yourself and Others 당신 자신과 타인을 소개하기

Getting Someone's Attention
누군가의 주목을 끌기

Expressing Gratitude
감사 표시 하기

Saying You Don't Understand
이해가 안됨을 얘기하기

Calling Someone on the Telephone
전화로 누군가와 통화하기

안녕하세요?	12	Hello. My name is ..../ Hi. I'm ....
제 이름은 …입니다.		
만나서 반갑니다.	13	Nice to meet you.
저도 만나뵈서 좋습니다.	14	Nice to meet you, too.
…을 소개하겠습니다./	15	I'd like to introduce ..../ This is ....
이분은 …입니다.		
실례합니다.	16	Excuse me.
질문 하나 해도 되겠습니까?	17	May I ask a question?
감사합니다.	18	Thank you. / Thanks.

천만에요.	19	You're welcome.
잘 이해가 안됩니다./	20	I don't understand. / Sorry. I don't understand.
미안합니다. 잘 이해가 안됩니다.		
다시 한번 얘기해주시겠어요?/	21	Can you please repeat that?/ Can you please say that again?
다시 한번 말해주시겠어요?		
안녕하세요. 저는 …입니다.	22	Hello. This is .... May I please speak to ....?
…와 통화할 수 있나요?		
예, 잠시 기다려주십시오.	23	Yes. Hold on a moment.
미안합니다.	24	I'm sorry. .... isn't here right now.
… 이 지 금 안 계십니다.		

Practice conversations with other students. Use all the expressions on pages 12 and 13.

날씨

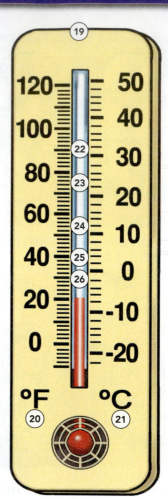

날씨	**Weather**			번개	**14** lightning
화창한	**1** sunny			천둥	**15** thunderstorm
흐린/구름 낀	**2** cloudy			눈보라	**16** snowstorm
맑은/개인	**3** clear			모래 폭풍	**17** dust storm
안개가 낀	**4** hazy			장기간의 혹서	**18** heat wave
안개가 자욱한	**5** foggy				
스모그가 많은	**6** smoggy			온도	**Temperature**
바람이 부는	**7** windy			온도계	**19** thermometer
습한/무더운 (후덥지근한)	**8** humid/muggy			화씨	**20** Fahrenheit
비가 오는	**9** raining			섭씨	**21** Centigrade/Celsius
이슬비가 내리는	**10** drizzling			더운	**22** hot
눈이 내리는	**11** snowing			따뜻한	**23** warm
우박이 내리는	**12** hailing			시원한	**24** cool
진눈깨비가 내리는	**13** sleeting			추운	**25** cold
				몹시 추운	**26** freezing

[1–13]
A. What's the weather like?
B. It's _____.

[14–18]
A. What's the weather forecast?
B. There's going to be __[14]__ /
a __[15–18]__ .

[20–26]
A. How's the weather?
B. It's __[22–26]__ .
A. What's the temperature?
B. It's . . . degrees __[20–21]__ .

What's the weather like today? What's the temperature?   What's the weather forecast for tomorrow?

숫자

Cardinal Numbers 기수

0 zero	11 eleven	21 twenty-one	101 one hundred (and) one
1 one	12 twelve	22 twenty-two	102 one hundred (and) two
2 two	13 thirteen	30 thirty	1,000 one thousand
3 three	14 fourteen	40 forty	10,000 ten thousand
4 four	15 fifteen	50 fifty	100,000 one hundred thousand
5 five	16 sixteen	60 sixty	1,000,000 one million
6 six	17 seventeen	70 seventy	1,000,000,000 one billion
7 seven	18 eighteen	80 eighty	
8 eight	19 nineteen	90 ninety	
9 nine	20 twenty	100 one hundred	
10 ten			

A. How old are you?
B. I'm _____ years old.

A. How many people are there in your family?
B. _____.

Ordinal Numbers 서수

1st first	11th eleventh	21st twenty-first	101st one hundred (and) first
2nd second	12th twelfth	22nd twenty-second	102nd one hundred (and) second
3rd third	13th thirteenth	30th thirtieth	1,000th one thousandth
4th fourth	14th fourteenth	40th fortieth	10,000th ten thousandth
5th fifth	15th fifteenth	50th fiftieth	100,000th one hundred thousandth
6th sixth	16th sixteenth	60th sixtieth	1,000,000th one millionth
7th seventh	17th seventeenth	70th seventieth	1,000,000,000th one billionth
8th eighth	18th eighteenth	80th eightieth	
9th ninth	19th nineteenth	90th ninetieth	
10th tenth	20th twentieth	100th one hundredth	

A. What floor do you live on?
B. I live on the _____ floor.

A. Is this your first trip to our country?
B. No. It's my _____ trip.

How many students are there in your class?

How many people are there in your country?

What were the names of your teachers in elementary school?
(My *first*-grade teacher was Ms./Mrs./Mr. . . .)

시간

two o'clock

two fifteen/
a quarter after *two*

two thirty/
half past *two*

two forty-five/
a quarter to *three*

two oh five

two twenty/
twenty after *two*

two forty/
twenty to *three*

two fifty-five/
five to *three*

A. What time is it?
B. It's _____.

A. What time does the movie begin?
B. At _____.

two A.M.

two P.M.

noon/
twelve noon

midnight/
twelve midnight

A. When does the train leave?
B. At _____.

A. What time will we arrive?
B. At _____.

Tell about your daily schedule:
    What do you do? When?
    (I get up at _____. I ....)

Do you usually have enough time to do things, or do you "run out of time"? Tell about it.

Tell about the use of time in different cultures or countries you know:
    Do people arrive on time for work? appointments? parties?
    Do trains and buses operate exactly on schedule?
    Do movies and sports events begin on time?
    Do workplaces use time clocks or timesheets to record employees' work hours?

Coins 동전
화폐

Name	Value	Written as:	
1 penny	one cent	1¢	$ .01
2 nickel	five cents	5¢	$ .05
3 dime	ten cents	10¢	$ .10
4 quarter	twenty-five cents	25¢	$ .25
5 half dollar	fifty cents	50¢	$ .50
6 silver dollar	one dollar		$1.00

A. How much is a **penny** worth?
B. A **penny** is worth **one cent**.

A. *Soda* costs *ninety-five cents.* Do you have enough change?
B. Yes. I have a/two/three _____(s) and . . . .

Currency 지폐

Name	We sometimes say:	Value	Written as:
7 (one-) dollar bill	a one	one dollar	$ 1.00
8 five-dollar bill	a five	five dollars	$ 5.00
9 ten-dollar bill	a ten	ten dollars	$ 10.00
10 twenty-dollar bill	a twenty	twenty dollars	$ 20.00
11 fifty-dollar bill	a fifty	fifty dollars	$ 50.00
12 (one-) hundred dollar bill	a hundred	one hundred dollars	$100.00

A. I'm going to the supermarket. Do you have any cash?
B. I have a **twenty-dollar bill**.
A. **Twenty dollars** is enough. Thanks.

A. Can you change a **five-dollar bill**/a **five**?
B. Yes. I have *five* one-dollar bills/*five* ones.

Written as:	We say:
$1.30	a dollar and thirty cents
	a dollar thirty
$2.50	two dollars and fifty cents
	two fifty
$56.49	fifty-six dollars and forty-nine cents
	fifty-six forty-nine

Tell about some things you usually buy. What do they cost?

Name and describe the coins and currency in your country. What are they worth in U.S. dollars?

달력

2012
JANUARY

SUN	MON	TUE	WED	THU	FRI	SAT
6	7	8	9	10	11	12
1	2	3	4	5	6	7
8	9	10	11	12	13	14
15	16	17	18	19	20	21
22	23	24	25	26	27	28
29	30	31				

13 JAN 14 FEB 15 MAR 16 APR
17 MAY 18 JUN 19 JUL 20 AUG
21 SEP 22 OCT 23 NOV 24 DEC

25 1/3/12

JAN 3 2012

26

HAPPY 25th
27

28 APPOINTMENT
Charles Wong, M.D.
Date: *February 21*
Time: *3:00 PM*

연도	**1**	year
월	**2**	month
주간	**3**	week
일	**4**	day
주말	**5**	weekend

요일 Days of the Week

일요일	**6**	Sunday
월요일	**7**	Monday
화요일	**8**	Tuesday
수요일	**9**	Wednesday
목요일	**10**	Thursday
금요일	**11**	Friday
토요일	**12**	Saturday

월 Months of the Year

1월	**13**	January
2월	**14**	February
3월	**15**	March
4월	**16**	April
5월	**17**	May
6월	**18**	June
7월	**19**	July
8월	**20**	August
9월	**21**	September
10월	**22**	October
11월	**23**	November
12월	**24**	December

2012년	**25**	January 3, 2012
1월 3일		January third, two thousand twelve
생일	**26**	birthday
기념일	**27**	anniversary
약속	**28**	appointment

A. What year is it?
B. It's _____.

[13–24]
A. What month is it?
B. It's _____.

[6–12]
A. What day is it?
B. It's _____.

A. What's today's date?
B. It's _____.

[26–28]
A. When is your _____?
B. It's on _____.

Which days of the week do you go to work/school?
(I go to work/school on _____.)

What do you do on the weekend?

What is your date of birth?
(I was born on ...*month day, year*....)

What's your favorite day of the week? Why?

What's your favorite month of the year? Why?

시간 표현과 계절

어제	**1**	yesterday	오늘 오후	**13**	this afternoon	일주일에 세번	**25**	three times a week
오늘	**2**	today	오늘 저녁	**14**	this evening	매일	**26**	every day
내일	**3**	tomorrow	오늘 밤	**15**	tonight			
아침	**4**	morning	내일 아침	**16**	tomorrow morning	계절		**Seasons**
오후	**5**	afternoon	내일 오후	**17**	tomorrow afternoon	봄	**27**	spring
저녁	**6**	evening	내일 저녁	**18**	tomorrow evening	여름	**28**	summer
밤	**7**	night	내일 밤	**19**	tomorrow night	가을	**29**	fall/autumn
어제 아침	**8**	yesterday morning	지난 주	**20**	last week	겨울	**30**	winter
어제 오후	**9**	yesterday afternoon	이번 주	**21**	this week			
어제 저녁	**10**	yesterday evening	다음 주	**22**	next week			
어제 밤	**11**	last night	일주일에 한번	**23**	once a week			
오늘 아침	**12**	this morning	일주일에 두번	**24**	twice a week			

What did you do yesterday morning/afternoon/evening? What did you do last night?

What are you going to do tomorrow morning/afternoon/evening/night?

What did you do last week?

What are your plans for next week?

How many times a week do you have English class?/go to the supermarket?/exercise?

What's your favorite season? Why?

주거 형태와 지역 사회 종류

아파트	**1**	apartment building	대피소	**9**	shelter
단독주택	**2**	house	농장	**10**	farm
2세대 주택	**3**	duplex/two-family house	대목장	**11**	ranch
연립주택	**4**	townhouse/townhome	선상주택	**12**	houseboat
콘도	**5**	condominium/condo	도시	**13**	the city
기숙사	**6**	dormitory/dorm	교외	**14**	the suburbs
이동주택	**7**	mobile home	시골	**15**	the country
요양원	**8**	nursing home	도심지	**16**	a town/village

A. Where do you live?

B. I live {
in a/an _____ [1–9] .
on a _____ [10–12] .
in _____ [13–16] .
}

[1–12]

A. Town Taxi Company.
B. Hello. Please send a taxi to
.....*(address)*.....
A. Is that a house or an apartment building?
B. It's a/an _____.
A. All right. We'll be there right away.

[1–12]

A. This is the Emergency Operator.
B. Please send an ambulance to
.....*(address)*.....
A. Is that a private home?
B. It's a/an _____.
A. What's your name and telephone number?
B. ....

Tell about people you know and where they live.

Discuss:
Who lives in dormitories?
Who lives in nursing homes?
Who lives in shelters?
Why?

거실

책장	1	bookcase	벽	10	wall	소파	20	sofa / couch
사진	2	picture / photograph	천장	11	ceiling	화초	21	plant
그림	3	painting	커튼	12	drapes	응접실 탁자	22	coffee table
벽난로 선반	4	mantel	창문	13	window	융단	23	rug
벽난로	5	fireplace	2인용 소파	14	loveseat	램프	24	lamp
벽난로 가리개/	6	fireplace screen	벽 장식장	15	wall unit	램프 갓	25	lampshade
벽난로 스크린			스피커	16	speaker	구석 테이블	26	end table
DVD 재생기	7	DVD player	스테레오 시스템	17	stereo system	마루	27	floor
텔레비전	8	television / TV	잡지 보관함	18	magazine holder	마루 전기 스텐드	28	floor lamp
비디오 카세트	9	VCR / video	(장식용)쿠션,베개	19	(throw) pillow	안락의자	29	armchair
녹화기		cassette recorder						

A. Where are you?
B. I'm in the living room.
A. What are you doing?
B. I'm dusting* the **bookcase**.

* dusting / cleaning

A. You have a very nice living room!

B. Thank you.

A. Your _____ is / are beautiful!

B. Thank you for saying so.

A. Uh-oh! I just spilled coffee on your _____!

B. That's okay. Don't worry about it.

Tell about your living room.
(In my living room there's ....)

식당

식탁	**1**	(dining room) table	도자기/	**12**	china	식탁보	**23** tablecloth
식탁 의자	**2**	(dining room) chair	자기(그릇)			냅킨	**24** napkin
식기장	**3**	buffet	샐러드 주발	**13**	salad bowl	포크	**25** fork
쟁반	**4**	tray	서빙 주발	**14**	serving bowl	접시	**26** plate
찻주전자	**5**	teapot	서빙 접시	**15**	serving dish	나이프	**27** knife
커피 주전자	**6**	coffee pot	꽃병	**16**	vase	스푼	**28** spoon
설탕 주발	**7**	sugar bowl	양초	**17**	candle	주발	**29** bowl
크림 그릇/프림용기	**8**	creamer	촛대	**18**	candlestick	머그잔	**30** mug
(물)주전자/	**9**	pitcher	큰접시	**19**	platter	유리잔	**31** glass
(물, 음료 등을 담는)피처			버터 접시	**20**	butter dish	컵/잔	**32** cup
샹들리에	**10**	chandelier	소금통	**21**	salt shaker	받침 접시	**33** saucer
장식용 찬장/찬장	**11**	china cabinet	후추통	**22**	pepper shaker		

A. This **dining room table** is very nice.
B. Thank you. It was a gift from my *grandmother*.*

*grandmother / grandfather / aunt / uncle / . . .

[In a store]
A. May I help you?
B. Yes, please. Do you have _____s?*
A. Yes. _____s* are right over there.
B. Thank you.

*With 12, use the singular.

[At home]
A. Look at this old _____ I just bought!
B. Where did you buy it?
A. At a yard sale. How do you like it?
B. It's VERY unusual!

Tell about your dining room.
(In my dining room there's
.............)

침실

침대	**1** bed	침대커버	**10** bedspread	침대용 탁자	**19** night table/
침대 머리판	**2** headboard	이불	**11** comforter/quilt		nightstand
베개	**3** pillow	카펫	**12** carpet	거울	**20** mirror
베갯잇	**4** pillowcase	서랍장	**13** chest (of drawers)	보석함	**21** jewelry box
매트 커버	**5** fitted sheet	블라인드/햇볕 가리개	**14** blinds	경대	**22** dresser/
홑 이불	**6** (flat) sheet	커튼	**15** curtains		bureau
담요	**7** blanket	램프	**16** lamp	매트리스	**23** mattress
전기 담요	**8** electric blanket	자명종	**17** alarm clock	침대 스프링 박스	**24** box spring
먼지막이 주름 장식	**9** dust ruffle	시계 라디오	**18** clock radio	침대 프레임	**25** bed frame

A. Ooh! Look at that big bug!
B. Where?
A. It's on the **bed**!
B. I'LL get it.

[In a store]
A. Excuse me. I'm looking for a/an _____.*
B. We have some very nice _____s, and they're all on sale this week!
A. Oh, good!

* With 14 & 15, use: Excuse me. I'm looking for _____

[In a bedroom]
A. Oh, no! I just lost my contact lens!
B. Where?
A. I think it's on the _____.
B. I'll help you look.

Tell about your bedroom.
(In my bedroom there's ....)

부엌

냉장고	**1**	refrigerator	음식 찌꺼기	**14**	(garbage)	버너	**25**	burner
냉동실	**2**	freezer	처리기		disposal	오븐	**26**	oven
쓰레기통	**3**	garbage pail	행주	**15**	dish towel	토스터	**27**	toaster
전동 혼합기	**4**	(electric) mixer	식기 건조대	**16**	dish rack/	원두커피기	**28**	coffeemaker
찬장	**5**	cabinet			dish drainer	쓰레기 압축기	**29**	trash
종이 타올 걸이	**6**	paper towel holder	양념통 보관대	**17**	spice rack			compactor
커피 보관통	**7**	canister	전동 깡통따개	**18**	(electric) can	도마	**30**	cutting
조리대	**8**	(kitchen) counter			opener			board
식기 세척기용	**9**	dishwasher	믹서기	**19**	blender	요리책	**31**	cookbook
세제		detergent	오븐 토스터	**20**	toaster oven	식품 전동	**32**	food
주방용 세제	**10**	dishwashing liquid	전자 레인지	**21**	microwave (oven)	조리기구		processor
수도꼭지	**11**	faucet	냄비 집게	**22**	potholder	부엌 의자	**33**	kitchen chair
부엌 싱크대	**12**	(kitchen) sink	차 주전자	**23**	tea kettle	부엌 식탁	**34**	kitchen table
식기 세척기	**13**	dishwasher	스토브/레인지	**24**	stove/range	식탁 매트	**35**	placemat

A. I think we need a new **refrigerator**.
B. I think you're right.

[In a store]

A. Excuse me. Are your _____s still on sale?

B. Yes, they are. They're twenty percent off.

[In a kitchen]

A. When did you get this/these new _____(s)?

B. I got it/them last week.

Tell about your kitchen.
(In my kitchen there's ....)

곰인형	1	teddy bear
아기 모니터기	2	baby monitor/intercom
서랍장	3	chest (of drawers)
아기침대	4	crib
완충 패드	5	crib bumper/bumper pad
모빌	6	mobile
기저귀 테이블	7	changing table
신축성 유아복	8	stretch suit
기저귀 테이블 패드	9	changing pad
기저귀 쓰레기통	10	diaper pail

야간등	11	night light
장난감 상자	12	toy chest
헝겊 동물인형	13	stuffed animal
인형	14	doll
그네	15	swing
아기 놀이 울/플래이 팬	16	playpen
딸랑이	17	rattle
보행기	18	walker
흔들침대	19	cradle
간이 유모차	20	stroller

유모차	21	baby carriage
자동차용 안전의자	22	car seat/safety seat
아기 이동 의자	23	baby carrier
음식 보온기	24	food warmer
보조의자/부스터 체어	25	booster seat
아기의자	26	baby seat
유아용 식판 의자	27	high chair
유아용 이동침대	28	portable crib
유아용 변기	29	potty
유모 앞배낭	30	baby frontpack
유모 등배낭	31	baby backpack

A. Thank you for the **teddy bear**. It's a very nice gift.
B. You're welcome. Tell me, when are you due?
A. In a few more weeks.

A. That's a very nice _____. Where did you get it?
B. It was a gift from ....

A. Do you have everything you need before the baby comes?
B. Almost everything. We're still looking for a/an _____ and a/an _____.

Tell about your country:
What things do people buy for a new baby? Does a new baby sleep in a separate room, as in the United States?

욕실

쓰레기통	**1**	wastebasket	헤어 드라이기	**14**	hair dryer	방향제	**25** air freshener
욕실 화장대/수건장	**2**	vanity	선반	**15**	shelf	변기	**26** toilet
비누	**3**	soap	세탁물 광주리	**16**	hamper	변기 시트	**27** toilet seat
비누 받침대	**4**	soap dish	환풍기	**17**	fan	샤워	**28** shower
물비누통	**5**	soap dispenser	목욕 수건	**18**	bath towel	샤워기	**29** shower head
세면대	**6**	(bathroom) sink	수건	**19**	hand towel	샤워 커튼	**30** shower curtain
수도 꼭지	**7**	faucet	세수 수건	**20**	washcloth/ faceclotch	욕조	**31** bathtub/tub
약장	**8**	medicine cabinet				욕조용 고무매트	**32** rubber mat
거울	**9**	mirror	수건 걸이	**21**	towel rack	배수구	**33** drain
컵	**10**	cup	흡인식 하수관 청소기	**22**	plunger	스폰지	**34** sponge
칫솔	**11**	toothbrush				욕실 매트	**35** bath mat
칫솔 걸이	**12**	toothbrush holder	변기 청소용 솔	**23**	toilet brush	체중 계량기	**36** scale
전동 칫솔	**13**	electric toothbrush	두루마리 화장지	**24**	toilet paper		

A. Where's the **hair dryer**?
B. It's *on* the **vanity**.

A. Where's the **soap**?
B. It's *in* the **soap dish**.

A. Where's the **plunger**?
B. It's *next to* the **toilet brush**.

A. [Knock. Knock.] Did I leave my glasses in there?
B. Yes. They're on/in/next to the _____.

A. *Bobby?* You didn't clean up the bathroom! There's toothpaste on the _____, and there's powder all over the _____!
B. Sorry. I'll clean it up right away.

Tell about your bathroom. (In my bathroom there's …………..)

집 외부

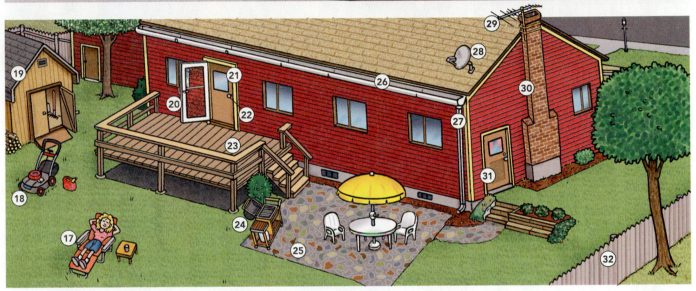

앞뜰	**Front Yard**				덧문/셔터	**12**	shutter			테라스	**23**	deck
가로등 기둥	**1**	lamppost			지붕	**13**	roof			바비큐 그릴	**24**	barbecue/
우체통	**2**	mailbox			차고	**14**	garage					(outdoor) grill
현관 앞길	**3**	front walk			차고 문	**15**	garage door			안뜰	**25**	patio
현관 계단	**4**	front steps			진입로	**16**	driveway			처마 물받이 홈통	**26**	gutter
현관	**5**	(front) porch								배수관	**27**	drainpipe
현관 덧문	**6**	storm door			뒷뜰	**Backyard**				위성방송 수신기	**28**	satellite dish
현관문	**7**	front door			야외용 의자	**17**	lawn chair			텔레비전 안테나	**29**	TV antenna
초인종	**8**	doorbell			잔디 깎는 기계	**18**	lawnmower			굴뚝	**30**	chimney
현관등	**9**	(front) light			연장(보관)창고	**19**	tool shed			옆문	**31**	side door
창문	**10**	window			방충문	**20**	screen door			울타리	**32**	fence
창 방충망	**11**	(window) screen			뒷문	**21**	back door					
					손잡이	**22**	door knob					

A. When are you going to repair the **lamppost**?
B. I'm going to repair it next Saturday.

[On the telephone]
A. Harry's Home Repairs.
B. Hello. Do you fix _____s?
A. No, we don't.
B. Oh, okay. Thank you.

[At work on Monday morning]
A. What did you do this weekend?
B. Nothing much. I repaired my _____ and my _____.

Do you like to repair things?
What things can you repair yourself?
What things can't you repair? Who repairs them?

아파트 건물

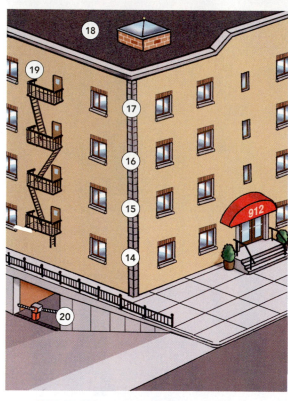

아파트를 찾기	**Looking for an Apartment**	이사 오기	**Moving In**	화재 비상 탈출구	**19** fire escape
아파트 광고/	**1** apartment ads/	이삿짐 트럭/	**8** moving truck/	옥내 주차장/	**20** parking
분야별 광고	classified ads	밴	moving van	차고	garage
아파트 목록	**2** apartment listings	이웃	**9** neighbor	발코니	**21** balcony
공실 표지판	**3** vacancy sign	빌딩 관리인	**10** building manager	안마당	**22** courtyard
		수위	**11** doorman	주차장	**23** parking lot
임대계약에 사인하기	**Signing a Lease**	열쇠	**12** key	주차 장소	**24** parking space
세입자	**4** tenant	자물쇠	**13** lock	수영장	**25** swimming
집주인	**5** landlord	1층	**14** first floor		pool
임대 계약	**6** lease	2층	**15** second floor	수압식 목욕탕	**26** whirlpool
보증금	**7** security deposit	3층	**16** third floor	휴지통	**27** trash bin
		4층	**17** fourth floor	에어컨	**28** air conditioner
		지붕	**18** roof		

로비 **Lobby**			복도 **Hallway**			지하 **Basement**		
인터폰 스피커	**29**	intercom/speaker	비상 계단/비상구	**38**	fire exit/ emergency stairway	창고	**43**	storage room
버저	**30**	buzzer	화재 경보기	**39**	fire alarm	창고 로커	**44**	storage locker
우편함	**31**	mailbox	스프링클러 장치	**40**	sprinkler system	세탁실	**45**	laundry room
엘리베이터/승강기	**32**	elevator	아파트 관리인	**41**	superintendent	보안문	**46**	security gate
계단	**33**	stairway	쓰레기 투입구	**42**	garbage chute/ trash chute			

현관 **Doorway**

방문객 확인 구멍	**34**	peephole
도어 체인	**35**	(door) chain
잠금쇠	**36**	dead-bolt lock
연기 탐지기	**37**	smoke detector

[19–46]
A. Is there a **fire escape**?
B. Yes, there is. Do you want to see the apartment?
A. Yes, I do.

[19–46]

   [Renting an apartment]

A. Let me show you around.
B. Okay.
A. This is the _____, and here's the _____.
B. I see.

[19–46]

   [On the telephone]

A. Mom and Dad? I found an apartment.
B. Good. Tell us about it.
A. It has a/an _____ and a/an _____.
B. That's nice. Does it have a/an _____?
A. Yes, it does.

Do you or someone you know live in an apartment building? Tell about it.

집 문제점들 및 보수

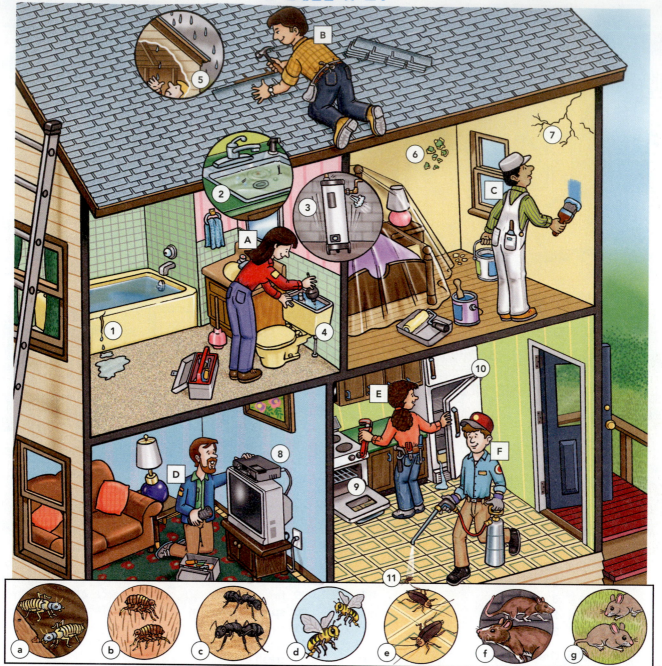

배관공	**A**	**plumber**
욕조가 샙니다.	**1**	The bathtub is leaking.
싱크대가 막혔습니다.	**2**	The sink is clogged.
온수 히터기가 작동하지 않습니다.	**3**	The hot water heater isn't working.
변기가 망가졌습니다.	**4**	The toilet is broken.
지붕보수공	**B**	**roofer**
지붕이 샙니다.	**5**	The roof is leaking.
집 페인트공	**C**	**(house) painter**
페인트가 벗겨집니다.	**6**	The paint is peeling.
벽이 금이 갔습니다.	**7**	The wall is cracked.
케이블 TV 회사	**D**	**cable TV company**
케이블 TV가 나오지 않습니다.	**8**	The cable TV isn't working.

가전제품 수리공	**E**	**appliance repairperson**
스토브가 작동하지 않습니다.	**9**	The stove isn't working.
냉장고가 망가졌습니다.	**10**	The refrigerator is broken.
방역원	**F**	**exterminator/ pest control specialist**
부엌에 ____ 가 있습니다.	**11**	There are ____ in the kitchen.
흰개미	**a**	termites
벼룩	**b**	fleas
개미	**c**	ants
벌	**d**	bees
바퀴벌레	**e**	cockroaches
쥐	**f**	rats
생쥐	**g**	mice

열쇠 수리공/자물쇠 수리공 G locksmith
자물쇠가 망가졌습니다. 12 The lock is broken.

전기 기사 H electrician
현관 등이 들어오지 않습니다. 13 The front light doesn't go on.
초인종이 울리지 않습니다. 14 The doorbell doesn't ring.
거실 전기가 나갔습니다. 15 The power is out in the living room.

굴뚝 청소부 I chimneysweep
굴뚝이 지저분합니다. 16 The chimney is dirty.

집 수리공 J home repairperson/"handyman"
욕실 타일이 떨어질 것 같습니다. 17 The tiles in the bathroom are loose.

목수 K carpenter
계단이 망가졌습니다. 18 The steps are broken.
문이 열리지 않습니다. 19 The door doesn't open.

냉난방 설비 L heating and air conditioning service
난방 시스템이 고장 났습니다. 20 The heating system is broken.
에어컨이 작동되지 않습니다. 21 The air conditioning isn't working.

A. What's the matter?
B. ___[1–21]___.
A. I think we should call a/an ___[A–L]___.

[1–21]
A. I'm having a problem in my apartment/house.
B. What's the problem?
A. _____.

[A–L]
A. Can you recommend a good _____?
B. Yes. You should call ....

What do you do when there are problems in your home? Do you fix things yourself, or do you call someone?

집청소하기

바닥을 쓸다	**A** sweep the floor	양복 솔	**3** whisk broom	걸레	**15** dust cloth
진공 청소기로	**B** vacuum	양탄자 청소기	**4** carpet sweeper	깃털 총채/	**16** feather duster
청소하다		진공 청소기	**5** vacuum (cleaner)	먼지털이	
마루를 걸레질하다	**C** mop the floor	진공 청소기	**6** vacuum cleaner	마루용 왁스	**17** floor wax
창문을 닦다	**D** wash the windows	부속품	attachments	가구 광택제	**18** furniture polish
먼지를 털다	**E** dust	진공 청소기 봉지	**7** vacuum cleaner bag	세제	**19** cleanser
마루에 왁스칠하다	**F** wax the floor	휴대용 진공 청소기	**8** hand vacuum	세탁솔/	**20** scrub brush
가구를 광택내다	**G** polish the furniture	자루걸레	**9** (dust) mop/(dry) mop	수세미	
욕실을 청소하다	**H** clean the bathroom	스폰지 자루걸레	**10** (sponge) mop	스폰지	**21** sponge
쓰레기를 내다버리다	**I** take out the garbage	자루 물걸레	**11** (wet) mop	양동이	**22** bucket/pail
빗자루	**1** broom	종이 타올	**12** paper towels	쓰레기통	**23** trash can/
쓰레받기	**2** dustpan	유리창 세제	**13** window cleaner		garbage can
		암모니아	**14** ammonia	재활용 상자	**24** recycling bin

[A–I]
A. What are you doing?
B. I'm **sweep**ing **the floor.**

[1–24]
A. I can't find the **broom.**
B. Look over there!

[1–12, 15, 16, 20–24]
A. Excuse me. Do you sell _____(s)?
B. Yes. They're at the back of the store.
A. Thanks.

[13, 14, 17–19]
A. Excuse me. Do you sell _____?
B. Yes. It's at the back of the store.
A. Thanks.

What household cleaning chores do people do in your home? What things do they use?

가정용품

야드 자	1	yardstick
파리채	2	fly swatter
흡인식 하수관 청소기	3	plunger
손전등	4	flashlight
연장 코드	5	extension cord
줄자	6	tape measure
접사다리	7	step ladder
쥐덫	8	mousetrap
마스킹 테이프/보호테이프	9	masking tape

전선 테이프	10	electrical tape
도관 테이프	11	duct tape
건전지	12	batteries
전구	13	lightbulbs/bulbs
퓨즈	14	fuses
오일	15	oil
접착제/풀	16	glue
작업용 장갑	17	work gloves
살충 분무기	18	bug spray/insect spray

바퀴벌레약	19	roach killer
사포/샌드페이퍼	20	sandpaper
페인트	21	paint
페인트 희석액	22	paint thinner
페인트붓	23	paintbrush/brush
(납작한) 페인트 그릇	24	paint pan
페인트 롤러	25	paint roller
분무기	26	spray gun

A. I can't find the **yardstick**!
B. Look in the utility cabinet.
A. I did.
B. Oh! Wait a minute! I lent the **yardstick** to the neighbors.

[1–8, 23–26]
A. I'm going to the hardware store.
   Can you think of anything we need?
B. Yes. We need a/an _____.
A. Oh, that's right.

[9–22]
A. I'm going to the hardware store.
   Can you think of anything we need?
B. Yes. We need _____.
A. Oh, that's right.

What home supplies do you have? How and when do you use each one?

도구와 철물

망치	**1** hammer	끌/정	**11** chisel	회전톱	**21** circular saw/
나무메	**2** mallet	스크레이퍼	**12** scraper		power saw
도끼	**3** ax	전선 피복 제거기	**13** wire stripper	전동 사포	**22** power sander
톱	**4** saw/handsaw	드릴	**14** hand drill	전동 천공기	**23** router
쇠톱/활톱	**5** hacksaw	바이스	**15** vise	전선	**24** wire
수평기	**6** level	집게	**16** pliers	못	**25** nail
드라이버	**7** screwdriver	공구상자/연장상자	**17** toolbox	따리쇠	**26** washer
십자 드라이버	**8** Phillips screwdriver	대패	**18** plane	너트	**27** nut
렌치	**9** wrench	전기드릴/천공기	**19** electric drill	나무나사	**28** wood screw
멍키렌치	**10** monkey wrench/	드릴 날	**20** (drill) bit	기계나사	**29** machine screw
	pipe wrench			볼트	**30** bolt

A. Can I borrow your **hammer**?
B. Sure.
A. Thanks.

With 25–30, use: Could I borrow some _____s?

[1–15, 17–24]

A. Where's the _____?
B. It's on/next to/near/over/under the _____.

[16, 25–30]

A. Where are the _____s?
B. They're on/next to/near/over/under the _____.

Do you like to work with tools? What tools do you have in your home?

정원관리 도구 및 활동

잔디를 깎다	**A**	mow the lawn	잔디 깎는 기계	**1**	lawnmower	노즐/호스 주둥이	**11** nozzle
야채를 심다	**B**	plant vegetables	휘발유통	**2**	gas can	스프링클러/살수기	**12** sprinkler
꽃을 심다	**C**	plant flowers	끝선 마무리기	**3**	line trimmer	물뿌리개	**13** watering can
꽃에 물을 주다	**D**	water the flowers	삽	**4**	shovel	갈퀴/써레	**14** rake
나뭇잎을 긁어모으다	**E**	rake leaves	야채 종자	**5**	vegetable seeds	나뭇잎 청소기	**15** leaf blower
울타리를 다듬다	**F**	trim the hedge	괭이	**6**	hoe	뜰 쓰레기 봉투	**16** yard waste bag
덤불 가지를 잘라내다	**G**	prune the bushes	모종삽	**7**	trowel	울타리 전지가위	**17** (hedge) clippers
잡초를 뽑다	**H**	weed	일륜 손수레	**8**	wheelbarrow	울타리 다듬기	**18** hedge trimmer
			비료	**9**	fertilizer	전지가위	**19** pruning shears
			정원용 호스	**10**	(garden) hose	잡초기	**20** weeder

[A–H]
A. Hi! Are you busy?
B. Yes. I'm **mow**ing **the lawn**.

[1–20]
A. What are you looking for?
B. The **lawnmower**.

[A–H]
A. What are you going to do tomorrow?
B. I'm going to _____.

[1–20]
A. Can I borrow your _____?
B. Sure.

Do you ever work with any of these tools? Which ones? What do you do with them?

읍내 주변 장소 I

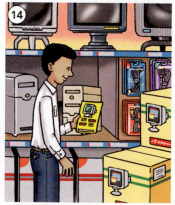

제과점	1	bakery	자동차 판매대리점	7	car dealership	의원/병원	11	clinic
은행	2	bank	카드 가게	8	card store	옷가게	12	clothing store
이발소	3	barber shop	탁아소/놀이방	9	child-care center/	커피숍	13	coffee shop
서점/책방	4	book store			day-care center	컴퓨터 판매점	14	computer store
버스 정거장/버스 터미널	5	bus station	세탁소	10	cleaners /	편의점	15	convenience store
사탕(과자)가게	6	candy store			dry cleaners	복사 센터	16	copy center

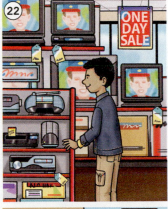

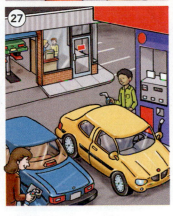
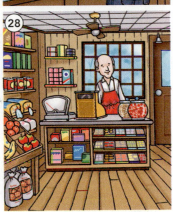

조제식품판매점	17	delicatessen/deli	가전제품 가게	22	electronics store	가구점	26	furniture store
백화점	18	department store	안경점	23	eye-care center/ optician	주유소	27	gas station/ service station
할인매장	19	discount store						
도넛 가게	20	donut shop	패스트 푸드 식당	24	fast-food restaurant	식품점	28	grocery store
약국	21	drug store/ pharmacy	꽃집	25	flower shop/florist			

A. Where are you going?
B. I'm going to the **bakery**.

A. Hi! How are you today?
B. Fine. Where are you going?
A. To the _____. How about you?
B. I'm going to the _____.

A. Oh, no! I can't find my wallet/purse!
B. Did you leave it at the _____?
A. Maybe I did.

Which of these places are in your neighborhood?
(In my neighborhood there's a/an ....)

읍내 주변 장소 II

미용실/미장원	1	hair salon
철물점	2	hardware store
헬스클럽	3	health club
병원	4	hospital
호텔	5	hotel
아이스크림 가게	6	ice cream shop

귀금속점	7	jewelry store
빨래방	8	laundromat
도서관	9	library
임산부 전문점	10	maternity shop
모텔	11	motel
극장	12	movie theater

레코드 가게	13	music store
손톱손질가게	14	nail salon
공원	15	park
애완동물 가게	16	pet shop/ pet store

사진인화점	17	photo shop
피자 가게	18	pizza shop
우체국	19	post office
식당	20	restaurant
학교	21	school
신발 가게	22	shoe store
쇼핑몰	23	(shopping) mall
슈퍼마켓	24	supermarket
완구점/장난감 가게	25	toy store
기차역	26	train station
여행사	27	travel agency
비디오 가게	28	video store

A. Where's the **hair salon**?
B. It's right over there.

A. Is there a/an _____ nearby?
B. Yes. There's a/an _____ around the corner.
A. Thanks.

A. Excuse me. Where's the _____?
B. It's down the street, next to the _____.
A. Thank you.

Which of these places are in your neighborhood?
(In my neighborhood there's a/an ....)

도시

법원	1	courthouse	시청	7	city hall	가로등	15	street light
택시	2	taxi / cab / taxicab	화재 경보함	8	fire alarm box	주차장 (외부)	16	parking lot
택시 승강장	3	taxi stand	우체통	9	mailbox	여자 주차 단속원	17	meter maid
택시 운전기사	4	taxi driver / cab driver	하수구	10	sewer	주차 미터기	18	parking meter
소화전	5	fire hydrant	경찰서	11	police station	쓰레기차	19	garbage truck
쓰레기통	6	trash container	교도소	12	jail	지하철	20	subway
			보도	13	sidewalk	지하철 역	21	subway station
			도로	14	street			

신문 가판대	**22** newsstand	연석	**29** curb	공중전화	**36** public telephone
교통신호등	**23** traffic light / traffic signal	주차장 건물/차고	**30** parking garage	도로 표지판	**37** street sign
교차로	**24** intersection	소방서	**31** fire station	맨홀	**38** manhole
경찰	**25** police officer	버스 정류장	**32** bus stop	오토바이	**39** motorcycle
횡단보도	**26** crosswalk	버스	**33** bus	행상인	**40** street vendor
보행자	**27** pedestrian	버스 운전기사	**34** bus driver	드라이브 스루 창	**41** drive-through window
아이스크림 트럭	**28** ice cream truck	사무실용 빌딩	**35** office building		

A. Where's the _____?
B. On/In/Next to/Between/Across from/ In front of/Behind/Under/Over the _____.

[An Election Speech]

If I am elected mayor, I'll take care of all the problems in our city. We need to do something about our _____s. We also need to do something about our _____s. And look at our _____s! We REALLY need to do something about THEM! We need a new mayor who can solve these problems. If I am elected mayor, we'll be proud of our _____s, _____s, and _____s again! Vote for me!

Go to an intersection in your city or town. What do you see? Make a list. Then tell about it.

사람과 신체 묘사

어린이-어린이들	**1**	**child-children**
아기	**2**	baby/infant
유아	**3**	toddler
소년	**4**	boy
소녀	**5**	girl
십대	**6**	teenager
어른	**7**	**adult**
남자 - 남자들	**8**	man–men
여자 - 여자들	**9**	woman–women
노인	**10**	senior citizen/ elderly person

나이	**age**
어린/젊은	**11**	young
중년의	**12**	middle-aged
나이 든/늙은	**13**	old/elderly
키	**height**
키가 큰	**14**	tall
평균 키	**15**	average height
키가 작은	**16**	short
몸무게	**weight**
뚱뚱한	**17**	heavy
평균 몸무게	**18**	average weight
마른	**19**	thin/slim
임신한	**20**	pregnant

육체적 장애가 있는	**21**	physically challenged
시각 장애가 있는	**22**	vision impaired
청각 장애가 있는	**23**	hearing impaired

머리 묘사하기 Describing Hair

긴	**24**	long
어깨까지 닿는	**25**	shoulder length
짧은	**26**	short
곧은	**27**	straight
웨이브가 있는	**28**	wavy
곱슬곱슬한	**29**	curly

검정색의	**30**	black
갈색의	**31**	brown
금발의	**32**	blond
빨강색의	**33**	red
회색의	**34**	gray

머리가 벗어진/ 대머리의	**35**	bald
턱수염	**36**	beard
콧수염	**37**	mustache

A. Tell me about *your brother*.
B. *He's a tall heavy boy* with *short curly brown* hair.

A. What does *your new boss* look like?
B. *She's average height*, and *she* has *long straight black* hair.

A. Can you describe *the person*?
B. *He's a tall thin middle-aged man.*
A. Anything else?
B. Yes. *He's bald*, and *he* has *a mustache*.

A. Can you describe *your grandmother*?
B. *She's a short thin elderly person* with *long wavy gray* hair.
A. Anything else?
B. Yes. *She's hearing impaired*.

Tell about yourself.

Tell about people in your family.

Tell about your favorite actor or actress or other famous person.

인물 및 사물 묘사하기

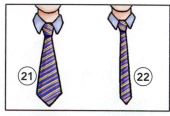

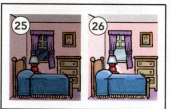
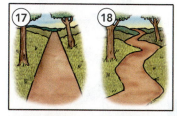

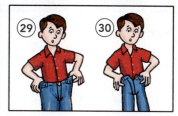
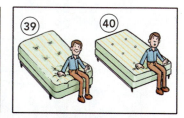

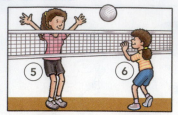

새로운-오래된	**1-2** new – old
어린-나이든	**3-4** young – old
키 큰-키 작은	**5-6** tall – short
긴-짧은	**7-8** long – short
큰-작은	**9-10** large/big – small/little
빠른-느린	**11-12** fast – slow
무거운/뚱뚱한-날씬한/마른	**13-14** heavy/fat – thin/skinny
무거운-가벼운	**15-16** heavy – light
곧은-구부러진	**17-18** straight – crooked
곧은-곱슬곱슬한	**19-20** straight – curly
넓은-좁은	**21-22** wide – narrow
두꺼운-얇은	**23-24** thick – thin

어두운-밝은	**25-26** dark – light
높은-낮은	**27-28** high – low
헐렁한-꼭 끼는	**29-30** loose – tight
좋은-나쁜	**31-32** good – bad
뜨거운-차가운	**33-34** hot – cold
깔끔한-지저분한	**35-36** neat – messy
깨끗한-더러운	**37-38** clean – dirty
부드러운-딱딱한	**39-40** soft – hard
쉬운-어려운	**41-42** easy – difficult/hard
매끄러운-거친	**43-44** smooth – rough
시끄러운-조용한	**45-46** noisy/loud – quiet
기혼의-미혼의	**47-48** married – single

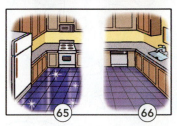

부유한-가난한 **49–50** rich/wealthy – poor	화려한-평범한/무난한 **63–64** fancy – plain	
예쁜-추한 **51–52** pretty/beautiful – ugly	빛나는-우중충한 **65–66** shiny – dull	
잘생긴-못생긴 **53–54** handsome – ugly	날카로운-무딘 **67–68** sharp – dull	
젖은-마른 **55–56** wet – dry	편안한-불편한 **69–70** comfortable – uncomfortable	
열려 있는-닫혀 있는 **57–58** open – closed	정직한-부정직한 **71–72** honest – dishonest	
가득찬-빈 **59–60** full – empty		
비싼-싼 **61–62** expensive – cheap/inexpensive		

[1–2]
A. Is your car **new**?
B. No. It's **old**.

1–2	Is your car _____?	25–26	Is the room _____?	49–50	Is your uncle _____?
3–4	Is he _____?	27–28	Is the bridge _____?	51–52	Is the witch _____?
5–6	Is your sister _____?	29–30	Are the pants _____?	53–54	Is the pirate _____?
7–8	Is his hair _____?	31–32	Are your neighbor's children _____?	55–56	Are the clothes _____?
9–10	Is their dog _____?	33–34	Is the water _____?	57–58	Is the door _____?
11–12	Is the train _____?	35–36	Is your desk _____?	59–60	Is the pitcher _____?
13–14	Is your friend _____?	37–38	Are the windows _____?	61–62	Is that restaurant _____?
15–16	Is the box _____?	39–40	Is the mattress _____?	63–64	Is the dress _____?
17–18	Is the road _____?	41–42	Is the homework _____?	65–66	Is your kitchen floor _____?
19–20	Is her hair _____?	43–44	Is your skin _____?	67–68	Is the knife _____?
21–22	Is the tie _____?	45–46	Is your neighbor _____?	69–70	Is the chair _____?
23–24	Is the line _____?	47–48	Is your sister _____?	71–72	Is he _____?

A. Tell me about your ....
B. He's/She's/It's/They're _____.

A. Do you have a/an _____ ....?
B. No. I have a/an _____ ....

Describe yourself.
Describe a person you know.
Describe some things in your home.
Describe some things in your community.

육체 상태와 감정 묘사하기

피곤한	1	tired
졸린	2	sleepy
지친	3	exhausted
병 난	4	sick / ill
더운	5	hot
추운	6	cold

배고픈	7	hungry
목마른	8	thirsty
배부른	9	full
행복한	10	happy
슬픈	11	sad / unhappy

비참한	12	miserable
신이 난	13	excited
실망한	14	disappointed
기분이 상한	15	upset
짜증난/ 귀찮은	16	annoyed

화난/성난	17	angry/mad
격노한	18	furious
정떨어진/	19	disgusted
메스꺼운		
좌절한	20	frustrated
놀란	21	surprised

경악한	22	shocked
외로운	23	lonely
고향을 그리워하는	24	homesick
초조한	25	nervous
걱정스러운	26	worried
겁먹은	27	scared/afraid

지루한	28	bored
자랑스러운	29	proud
당혹한	30	embarrassed
질투가 많은	31	jealous
혼란스러운	32	confused

A. You look _____.
B. I am. I'm VERY _____.

A. Are you _____?
B. No. Why do you ask? Do I LOOK _____?
A. Yes. You do.

What makes you happy? sad? mad?

What do you do when you feel nervous? annoyed?

Do you ever feel embarrassed? When?

과일

사과	**1**	apple	무화과 열매	**12**	fig	오렌지	**22**	orange
복숭아	**2**	peach	코코넛	**13**	coconut	귤	**23**	tangerine
서양배	**3**	pear	아보카도	**14**	avocado	포도	**24**	grapes
바나나	**4**	banana	머스크 멜론	**15**	cantaloupe	버찌/체리	**25**	cherries
요리용 바나나	**5**	plantain	감로 멜론	**16**	honeydew	말린 자두	**26**	prunes
자두	**6**	plum			(melon)	대추야자 열매	**27**	dates
살구	**7**	apricot	수박	**17**	watermelon	건포도	**28**	raisins
승도 복숭아	**8**	nectarine	파인애플	**18**	pineapple	견과류	**29**	nuts
키위	**9**	kiwi	그레이프프루트	**19**	grapefruit	나무딸기/라스베리	**30**	raspberries
파파야	**10**	papaya	레몬	**20**	lemon	블루베리	**31**	blueberries
망고	**11**	mango	라임	**21**	lime	딸기	**32**	strawberries

[1–23]
A. This **apple** is delicious!
    Where did you get it?
B. At *Sam's Supermarket*.

[24–32]
A. These **grapes** are delicious!
    Where did you get them?
B. At *Franny's Fruit Stand*.

A. I'm hungry. Do we have any fruit?
B. Yes. We have _____s* and
    _____s.*

* With 15–19, use:
   We have _____ and _____.

A. Do we have any more _____s?†
B. No. I'll get some more when I go
    to the supermarket.

† With 15–19 use:
   Do we have any more _____?

What are your favorite fruits?
Which fruits don't you like?

Which of these fruits grow where you live?

Name and describe other fruits you know.

야채

셀러리	1	celery
옥수수	2	corn
브로콜리	3	broccoli
꽃양배추	4	cauliflower
시금치	5	spinach
파슬리	6	parsley
아스파라거스	7	asparagus
가지	8	eggplant
양상추	9	lettuce
양배추	10	cabbage
중국 배추	11	bok choy
애호박	12	zucchini
도토리호박/에이콘 스콰시	13	acorn squash
버터호두호박	14	butternut squash

마늘	15	garlic
완두콩	16	pea
깍지콩	17	string bean/ green bean
리마콩	18	lima bean
검정콩	19	black bean
강낭콩	20	kidney bean
꼬마 양배추	21	brussels sprout
오이	22	cucumber
토마토	23	tomato
당근	24	carrot
무	25	radish
버섯	26	mushroom
솜엉겅퀴	27	artichoke

감자	28	potato
고구마	29	sweet potato
참마	30	yam
피망	31	green pepper/ sweet pepper
고추	32	red pepper
멕시코산 고추/ 할라페노 고추	33	jalapeño (pepper)
칠리 고추	34	chili pepper
사탕무	35	beet
양파	36	onion
파	37	scallion/ green onion
순무	38	turnip

A. What do we need from the supermarket?
B. We need **celery*** and **peas**.†

* 1–15   † 16–38

A. How do you like the
   ___[1–15]___ / ___[16–38]___s?
B. It's/They're delicious.

A. *Bobby*? Finish your vegetables!
B. But you KNOW I hate
   ___[1–15]___ / ___[16–38]___s!
A. I know. But it's/they're good for you!

Which vegetables do you like?
Which vegetables don't you like?

Which of these vegetables grow where you live?

Name and describe other vegetables you know.

육류, 가금 및 해산 식품

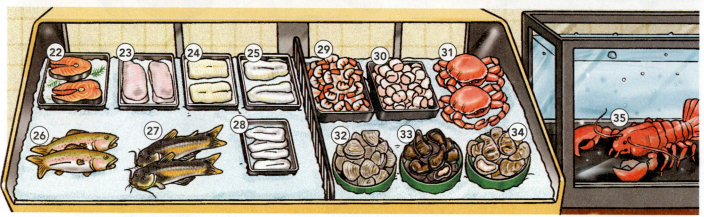

육류	**Meat**		가금류	**Poultry**		가자미	**25** flounder
스테이크용 고기	**1** steak		닭고기	**15** chicken		송어	**26** trout
다진 소고기	**2** ground beef		닭 가슴살	**16** chicken breasts		메기	**27** catfish
스튜용 쇠고기	**3** stewing beef		닭다리	**17** chicken legs/		서대기 생선토막	**28** filet of
로스트 비프	**4** roast beef			drumsticks			sole
갈비	**5** ribs		닭 날개	**18** chicken wings		패류	**SHELLFISH**
양다리	**6** leg of lamb		닭 넓적다리	**19** chicken thighs		새우	**29** shrimp
양 갈비살	**7** lamb chops		칠면조	**20** turkey		가리비	**30** scallops
양(소 내장의)	**8** tripe		오리고기	**21** duck		게	**31** crabs
간	**9** liver					대합	**32** clams
돼지고기	**10** pork		해산 식품	**Seafood**		홍합	**33** mussels
돼지 갈비살/돼지고기 토막	**11** pork chops		생선	**FISH**		굴	**34** oysters
소시지	**12** sausages		연어	**22** salmon		바닷가재	**35** lobster
햄	**13** ham		넙치	**23** halibut			
베이컨	**14** bacon		대구	**24** haddock			

A. I'm going to the supermarket. What do we need?
B. Please get some **steak**.
A. **Steak**? All right.

A. Excuse me. Where can I find _____?
B. Look in the _____ Section.
A. Thank you.

A. This/These _____ looks/
look very fresh!
B. Let's get some for dinner.

Do you eat meat, poultry, or seafood?
Which of these foods do you like?

Which of these foods are popular in your country?

유제품, 주스 및 음료수

유제품 Dairy Products

우유	1	milk
저지방 우유	2	low-fat milk
탈지유	3	skim milk
쵸코렛 우유	4	tchocolate milk
오렌지 쥬스*	5	orange juice*
치즈	6	cheese
버터	7	butter
마가린	8	margarine
산패유	9	sour cream
크림치즈	10	cream cheese
코티지 치즈	11	cottage cheese
요구르트/	12	yogurt
유산균 발효유		
두부*	13	tofu*
달걀	14	eggs

주스 Juices

사과 주스	15	apple juice
파인애플 주스	16	pineapple juice
자몽 주스	17	grapefruit juice
토마토 주스	18	tomato juice
포도 주스	19	grape juice
과일 펀치	20	fruit punch
주스팩	21	juice paks
분말음료	22	powdered drink mix

음료 Beverages

탄산음료/소다	23	soda
다이어트 탄산음료/ 무설탕 소다	24	diet soda
생수	25	bottled water

커피와 차 Coffee and Tea

커피	26	coffee
무카페인 커피	27	decaffeinated coffee/decaf
인스턴트 커피	28	instant coffee
차	29	tea
약초차/허브티	30	herbal tea
코코아	31	cocoa/hot chocolate mix

*오렌지 주스와 두부는 유제품이 아니지만 보통 이 부류에 넣는다.

A. I'm going to the supermarket to get some **milk**.
  Do we need anything else?
B. Yes. Please get some **apple juice**.

A. Excuse me. Where can I find _____?
B. Look in the _____ Section.
A. Thanks.

A. Look! _____ is/are on sale this week!
B. Let's get some!

Which of these foods do you like?

Which of these foods are good for you?

Which brands of these foods do you buy?

조제식품, 냉동식품 및 스낵식품

조제식품류 **Deli**	모차렐라 치즈	**11** mozzarella	냉동요리	**20** frozen dinners
로스트 비프 **1** roast beef	체더 치즈	**12** cheddar cheese	냉동 레모네이드	**21** frozen lemonade
볼로냐 소세지 **2** bologna	감자 샐러드	**13** potato salad	냉동 오렌지주스	**22** frozen orange juice
살라미 소시지 **3** salami	다진 양배추 샐러드	**14** cole slaw		
햄 **4** ham	마카로니 샐러드	**15** macaroni salad	간식류/스낵류	**Snack Foods**
칠면조 고기 **5** turkey	파스타 셀러드	**16** pasta salad	감자칩	**23** potato chips
콘비프 **6** corned beef	해물 샐러드	**17** seafood salad	토르티야 칩	**24** tortilla chips
양념훈제쇠고기 **7** pastrami			프레첼	**25** pretzels
스위스 치즈 **8** Swiss cheese	냉동식품류	**Frozen Foods**	견과(堅果)	**26** nuts
프로볼로네 치즈 **9** provolone	아이스크림	**18** ice cream	팝콘	**27** popcorn
아메리칸 치즈 **10** American cheese	냉동야채	**19** frozen vegetables		

A. Should we get some **roast beef**?
B. Good idea. And let's get some **potato salad**.

[1–17]
A. May I help you?
B. Yes, please. I'd like some _____.

[1–27]
A. Excuse me. Where is/are _____?
B. It's/They're in the _____ Section.

What kinds of snack foods are popular in your country?

Are frozen foods common in your country? What kinds of foods are in the Frozen Foods Section?

식료품

포장 제품류	**Packaged Goods**		양념	**Condiments**		제과류	**Baked Goods**
시리얼	**1** cereal		케첩	**15** ketchup		식빵	**30** bread
쿠키	**2** cookies		겨자	**16** mustard		롤빵	**31** rolls
크래커	**3** crackers		조미료	**17** relish		영국식 머핀	**32** English muffins
마카로니	**4** macaroni		오이절임/피클	**18** pickles		피타브레드	**33** pita bread
국수	**5** noodles		올리브	**19** olives		(납작한 빵)	
스파게티	**6** spaghetti		소금	**20** salt		케이크	**34** cake
쌀	**7** rice		후추	**21** pepper			
			양념	**22** spices		제과 재료	**Baking Products**
통조림류	**Canned Goods**		간장	**23** soy sauce		밀가루	**35** flour
수프	**8** soup		마요네즈	**24** mayonnaise		설탕	**36** sugar
참치	**9** tuna (fish)		식용유	**25** (cooking) oil		케이크 가루	**37** cake mix
야채 통조림	**10** (canned)		올리브유	**26** olive oil			
	vegetables		살사 소스	**27** salsa			
과일 통조림	**11** (canned) fruit		식초	**28** vinegar			
			샐러드 드레싱	**29** salad			
잼과 젤리	**Jams and Jellies**			dressing			
잼	**12** jam						
젤리	**13** jelly						
땅콩버터	**14** peanut butter						

A. I got **cereal** and **soup**. What else is on the shopping list?
B. **Ketchup** and **bread**.

A. Excuse me. I'm looking for _____.
B. It's/They're next to the _____.

A. Pardon me. I'm looking for _____.
B. It's/They're between the _____ and the _____.

Which of these foods do you like?

Which brands of these foods do you buy?

가사 용품, 아기 용품 및 애완동물 먹이

종이 제품들	**Paper Products**		가사 용품	**Household Items**		아기 용품	**Baby Products**
냅킨	**1** napkins		샌드위치 백	**8** sandwich bags		아기용 시리얼	**15** baby cereal
종이 컵	**2** paper cups		쓰레기 봉투	**9** trash bags		이유식	**16** baby food
티슈	**3** tissues		비누	**10** soap		분유	**17** formula
빨대	**4** straws		물 비누/액체 비누	**11** liquid soap		물휴지	**18** wipes
종이 접시	**5** paper plates		은박지	**12** aluminum foil		일회용 기저귀	**19** (disposable) diapers
종이 타월	**6** paper towels		비닐 랩	**13** plastic wrap		**애완동물 먹이**	**Pet Food**
화장지	**7** toilet paper		납지/왁스종이/파라핀	**14** waxed paper		고양이 먹이	**20** cat food
			종이			개 먹이	**21** dog food

A. Excuse me. Where can I find **napkins**?
B. **Napkins**? Look in Aisle 4.

[7, 10–17, 20, 21]
A. We forgot to get _____!
B. I'll get it. Where is it?
A. It's in Aisle _____.

[1–6, 8, 9, 18, 19]
A. We forgot to get _____!
B. I'll get them. Where are they?
A. They're in Aisle _____.

What do you need from the supermarket?
Make a complete shopping list!

슈퍼마켓

통로	**1**	aisle	포장 직원	**14** bagger / packer
손님/고객	**2**	shopper / customer	신속 계산대	**15** express checkout (line)
장바구니	**3**	shopping basket	타블로이드 (신문)	**16** tabloid (newspaper)
계산대 줄	**4**	checkout line	잡지	**17** magazine
계산대	**5**	checkout counter	스캐너	**18** scanner
컨베이어 벨트	**6**	conveyor belt	비닐 봉지	**19** plastic bag
금전등록기	**7**	cash register	농산물	**20** produce
쇼핑 카트	**8**	shopping cart	점장	**21** manager
껌	**9**	(chewing) gum	점원	**22** clerk
사탕	**10**	candy	저울	**23** scale
쿠폰	**11**	coupons	깡통 회수기	**24** can-return machine
계산원	**12**	cashier	병 회수기	**25** bottle-return machine
종이 봉지	**13**	paper bag		

[1–8, 11–19, 21–25]
A. This is a gigantic supermarket!
B. It is! Look at all the **aisle**s!

[9, 10, 20]
A. This is a gigantic supermarket!
B. It is. Look at all the **produce**!

Where do you usually shop for food? Do you go to a supermarket, or do you go to a small grocery store? Describe the place where you shop.

Describe the differences between U.S. supermarkets and food stores in your country.

용기들과 질량

봉지	**1** bag	결구 (양배추의)/포기	**9** head	한 자루(초콜릿)	**16** stick
병	**2** bottle	병	**10** jar	튜브	**17** tube
상자	**3** box	덩어리	**11** loaf–loaves	파인트 (약 0.57 리터)	**18** pint
다발/송이	**4** bunch	갑	**12** pack	쿼트 (1.14 리터)	**19** quart
깡통 /캔	**5** can	봉지	**13** package	반 갤런	**20** half-gallon
카톤 팩	**6** carton	롤	**14** roll	갤런 (3.78531리터)	**21** gallon
통	**7** container	여섯개 들이 팩	**15** six-pack	리터	**22** liter
다스/열두개	**8** dozen*			파운드 (453 그램)	**23** pound

* "a dozen eggs," NOT "a dozen of eggs"

A. Please get a **bag** of *flour* when you go to the supermarket.
B. A **bag** of *flour*? Okay.

A. Please get two **bottles** of *ketchup* when you go to the supermarket.
B. Two **bottles** of *ketchup*? Okay.

[At home]
A. What did you get at the supermarket?
B. I got _____, _____, and _____.

[In a supermarket]
A. Is this the express checkout line?
B. Yes, it is. Do you have more than eight items?
A. No. I only have _____, _____, and _____.

Open your kitchen cabinets and refrigerator. Make a list of all the things you find.

What do you do with empty bottles, jars, and cans? Do you recycle them, reuse them, or throw them away?

측량 단위

 티 스푼 teaspoon
tsp.

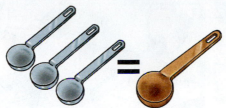 테이블 스푼 tablespoon
Tbsp.

 온스 1 (fluid) ounce
1 fl. oz.

 컵 cup
c.
8 fl. ozs.

 파인트 pint
pt.
16 fl. ozs.

 쿼트 (1.14 리터) quart
qt.
32 fl. ozs.

  갤런 (3.78531리터) gallon
gal.
128 fl. ozs.

A. How much water should I put in?
B. The recipe says to add one _____ of water.

A. This fruit punch is delicious! What's in it?
B. Two _____s of apple juice, three _____s
   of orange juice, and a _____ of grape juice.

온스 an ounce

oz.

1/4 파운드 a quarter
of a pound
1/4 lb.
4 ozs.

1/2 파운드 half a
pound
1/2 lb.
8 ozs.

3/4 파운드 three-quarters
of a pound
3/4 lb.
12 ozs.

파운드 a pound

lb.
16 ozs.

A. How much roast beef would you like?
B. I'd like _____, please.
A. Anything else?
B. Yes. Please give me _____ of Swiss cheese.

A. This chili tastes very good! What did you put
   in it?
B. _____ of ground beef, _____ of beans, _____ of
   tomatoes, and _____ of chili powder.

음식 준비 및 조리법

자르다	**1**	cut (up)
다지다	**2**	chop (up)
얇게 썰다	**3**	slice
갈다	**4**	grate
벗기다	**5**	peel
깨다	**6**	break
휘젓다	**7**	beat
젓다	**8**	stir
붓다	**9**	pour

첨가하다	**10**	add
____ 과 ____ 을 혼합하다	**11**	combine ____ and ____
____ 과 ____ 을 섞다	**12**	mix ____ and ____
____ 에 ____ 을 넣다	**13**	put ____ in ____
요리하다	**14**	cook
굽다	**15**	bake
삶다/데치다	**16**	boil
굽다	**17**	broil
찌다	**18**	steam

튀기다	**19**	fry
기름에 살짝 튀기다	**20**	saute
약불로 끓이다	**21**	simmer
(오븐에)굽다	**22**	roast
(불 위에/석쇠에)	**23**	barbecue / grill
굽다		
볶다	**24**	stir-fry
전자레인지로 조리하다	**25**	microwave

A. Can I help you?
B. Yes. Please **cut up** the vegetables.

[1–25]
A. What are you doing?
B. I'm _____ing the ....

[14–25]
A. How long should I _____ the ....?
B. _____ the .... for .... minutes/seconds.

What's your favorite recipe? Give instructions and use the units of measure on page 57. For example:

Mix a cup of flour and two tablespoons of sugar.
Add half a pound of butter.
Bake at 350° (degrees) for twenty minutes.

부엌 용품들 및 요리 기구

아이스크림 국자	**1** ice cream scoop	뒤집개/프라이	**13** spatula	밀대/밀방망이	**25** rolling pin
깡통 따개	**2** can opener	증기찜 받침대	**14** steamer	파이 굽는 용기	**26** pie plate
병따개	**3** bottle opener	칼	**15** knife	과도	**27** paring knife
야채 껍질 깎기	**4** (vegetable) peeler	마늘 압착기	**16** garlic press	쿠키 시트	**28** cookie sheet
달걀 거품기	**5** (egg) beater	강판	**17** grater	쿠키 절편판	**29** cookie cutter
뚜껑	**6** lid/cover/top	찜냄비	**18** casserole dish	섞는 주발	**30** (mixing) bowl
냄비/솥	**7** pot	오븐용 구이판	**19** roasting pan	거품기	**31** whisk
프라이팬	**8** frying pan/skillet	고기 구이대	**20** roasting rack	계량컵	**32** measuring cup
이중 냄비	**9** double boiler	고기 베는 칼	**21** carving knife	계량스푼	**33** measuring spoon
중국 냄비	**10** wok	소스 냄비	**22** saucepan	케익 굽는 용기	**34** cake pan
국자	**11** ladle	물 거르개	**23** colander	나무 스푼	**35** wooden spoon
체	**12** strainer	주방 타이머	**24** kitchen timer		

A. Could I possibly borrow your **ice cream scoop**?
B. Sure. I'll be happy to lend you my **ice cream scoop**.
A. Thanks.

A. What are you looking for?
B. I can't find the _____.
A. Look in that drawer/in that cabinet/ on the counter/next to the _____/ ....

[A Commercial]
Come to *Kitchen World*! We have everything you need for your kitchen, from _____s and _____s, to _____s and _____s. Are you looking for a new _____? Is it time to throw out your old _____? Come to *Kitchen World* today! We have everything you need!

What kitchen utensils and cookware do you have in your kitchen?

Which things do you use very often?

Which things do you rarely use?

패스트 푸드

햄버거	**1**	hamburger
치즈버거	**2**	cheeseburger
핫도그	**3**	hot dog
생선 샌드위치	**4**	fish sandwich
닭고기 샌드위치	**5**	chicken sandwich
닭튀김	**6**	fried chicken
감자 튀김/프렌치 프라이	**7**	french fries
나초	**8**	nachos
타코	**9**	taco
부리토	**10**	burrito
피자	**11**	slice of pizza
칠리 한 그릇	**12**	bowl of chili
샐러드	**13**	salad
아이스 크림	**14**	ice cream

요구르트아이스크림	**15**	frozen yogurt
밀크 셰이크	**16**	milkshake
탄산음료/소다	**17**	soda
뚜껑	**18**	lids
종이 컵	**19**	paper cups
빨대	**20**	straws
냅킨	**21**	napkins
프라스틱 주방용품	**22**	plastic utensils
케첩	**23**	ketchup
겨자	**24**	mustard
마요네즈	**25**	mayonnaise
조미료	**26**	relish
샐러드 드레싱	**27**	salad dressing

A. May I help you?
B. Yes. I'd like a/an ___[1–5, 9–17]___ /
an order of ___[6–8]___ .

A. Excuse me. We're almost out of
___[18–27]___ .
B. I'll get some more from the
supply room. Thanks for telling
me.

Do you go to fast-food restaurants? Which ones?
How often? What do you order?

Are there fast-food restaurants in your country?
Are they popular? What foods do they have?

커피샵과 샌드위치

도넛	**1** donut		초코릿 음료	**20** hot chocolate
머핀	**2** muffin		우유	**21** milk
베이글	**3** bagel		참치 샌드위치	**22** tuna fish sandwich
소형 롤빵/빈	**4** bun		달걀 샐러드 샌드위치	**23** egg salad sandwich
덴마크 빵과자	**5** danish/pastry		닭고기 샐러드 샌드위치	**24** chicken salad sandwich
비스킷	**6** biscuit		햄 치즈 샌드위치	**25** ham and cheese sandwich
초승달 롤빵/크루아상	**7** croissant		콘비프 샌드위치	**26** corned beef sandwich
달걀	**8** eggs		베이컨, 양상추, 토마토 샌드위치	**27** BLT/bacon, lettuce, and tomato sandwich
팬케이크	**9** pancakes		로스트 비프 샌드위치	**28** roast beef sandwich
와플	**10** waffles		흰빵	**29** white bread
토스트	**11** toast		통밀빵	**30** whole wheat bread
베이컨	**12** bacon		넓적 빵	**31** pita bread
소시지	**13** sausages		흑빵	**32** pumpernickel
홈프라이 (통감자튀김)	**14** home fries		호밀빵	**33** rye bread
커피	**15** coffee		롤빵	**34** a roll
무카페인 커피	**16** decaf coffee		바케트빵/긴 롤빵	**35** a submarine roll
차	**17** tea			
아이스 티/냉홍차	**18** iced tea			
레모네이드	**19** lemonade			

A. May I help you?
B. Yes. I'd like a ___[1–7]___/an order of ___[8–14]___, please.
A. Anything to drink?
B. Yes. I'll have a small/medium-size/large/extra-large ___[15–21]___.

A. I'd like a ___[22–28]___ on ___[29–35]___, please.
B. What do you want on it?
A. Lettuce/tomato/mayonnaise/mustard/...

Do you like these foods? Which ones? Where do you get them? How often do you have them?

식당

손님을 의자에 앉히다	A	seat the customers	보조 의자/부스터 체어	7	booster seat
물을 따르다	B	pour the water	메뉴	8	menu
주문을 받다	C	take the order	빵 바구니	9	bread basket
식사 음식를 차리다	D	serve the meal	웨이터의 조수	10	busperson
			웨이트리스	11	waitress/server
호스티스	1	hostess	웨이터	12	waiter/server
호스트	2	host	샐러드 바	13	salad bar
정찬 손님	3	diner/patron/customer	식당	14	dining room
칸막이 자리	4	booth	부엌	15	kitchen
식탁	5	table	요리사	16	chef
높은 의자	6	high chair			

[4-9]
A. Would you like a **booth**?
B. Yes, please.

[10-12]
A. Hello. My name is *Julie*, and I'll be
your **waitress** this evening.
B. Hello.

[1, 2, 13-16]
A. This restaurant has a
wonderful **salad bar**.
B. I agree.

식탁을 치우다	**E**	clear the table	수프 주발	**26** soup bowl
계산서를 지불하다	**F**	pay the check	물잔	**27** water glass
팁을 놓다	**G**	leave a tip	포도주잔	**28** wine glass
식탁을 차리다	**H**	set the table	컵	**29** cup
			컵 받침	**30** saucer
설거지실	**17**	dishroom	냅킨	**31** napkin
접시 닦는 사람	**18**	dishwasher		
쟁반	**19**	tray	**은제품 식기류**	**silverware**
후식 수레	**20**	dessert cart	샐러드용 포크	**32** salad fork
계산서	**21**	check	식사용 포크	**33** dinner fork
팁	**22**	tip	나이프	**34** knife
샐러드용 접시	**23**	salad plate	찻숟가락	**35** teaspoon
빵접시	**24**	bread-and-butter plate	수프 스푼	**36** soup spoon
디너접시	**25**	dinner plate	버터 나이프	**37** butter knife

[A–H]
A. Please _____.
B. All right. I'll _____ right away.

[23–37]
A. Excuse me. Where does the _____ go?
B. It goes {
to the left of the _____.
to the right of the _____.
on the _____.
between the _____ and the _____.
}

[1, 2, 10–12, 16, 18]
A. Do you have any job openings?
B. Yes. We're looking for a _____.

[23–37]
A. Excuse me. I dropped my _____.
B. That's okay. I'll get you another _____ from the kitchen.

Tell about a restaurant you know. Describe the place and the people. (Is the restaurant large or small? How many tables are there? How many people work there? Is there a salad bar? . . .)

식당 메뉴

프루트 칵테일	1	fruit cup/ fruit cocktail
토마토 주스	2	tomato juice
새우 칵테일	3	shrimp cocktail
닭 날개	4	chicken wings
나초	5	nachos
감자껍질요리/ 포테이토 스킨	6	potato skins
야채 샐러드	7	tossed salad/ garden salad
그리스 샐러드	8	Greek salad
시금치 샐러드	9	spinach salad
전채	10	antipasto (plate)
시저 샐러드	11	Caesar salad

미트 로프	12	meatloaf
쇠고기 구이/ 갈비살	13	roast beef/ prime rib
통닭구이	14	baked chicken
생선구이	15	broiled fish
스파게티와 미트 볼	16	spaghetti and meatballs
송아지고기 커트릿	17	veal cutlet
통감자 구이	18	a baked potato
으깬 감자요리	19	mashed potatoes
감자 튀김/ 프렌치 프라이	20	french fries
밥	21	rice
국수	22	noodles
모듬 야채	23	mixed vegetables

쵸코렛 케익	24	chocolate cake
애플파이	25	apple pie
아이스크림	26	ice cream
젤로	27	jello
푸딩	28	pudding
선디 아이스크림	29	ice cream sundae

[Ordering dinner]
A. May I take your order?
B. Yes, please. For the appetizer, I'd like the ____[1–6]____.
A. And what kind of salad would you like?
B. I'll have the ____[7–11]____.
A. And for the main course?
B. I'd like the ____[12–17]____, please.
A. What side dish would you like with that?
B. Hmm. I think I'll have ____[18–23]____.

[Ordering dessert]
A. Would you care for some dessert?
B. Yes. I'll have ____[24–28]____/an ____[29]____.

Tell about the food at a restaurant you know. What's on the menu?

What are some typical foods on the menus of restaurants in your country?

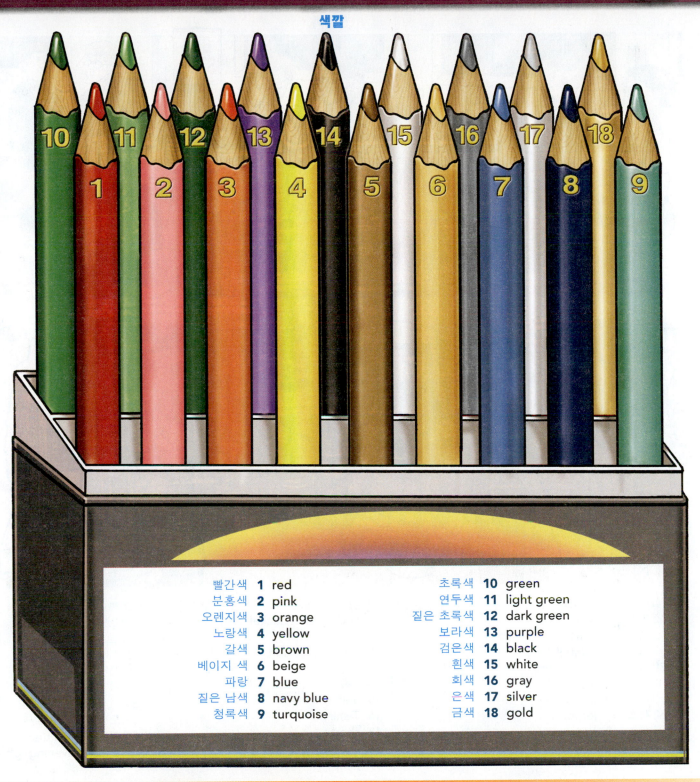

색깔

빨간색	**1** red	초록색	**10** green
분홍색	**2** pink	연두색	**11** light green
오렌지색	**3** orange	짙은 초록색	**12** dark green
노랑색	**4** yellow	보라색	**13** purple
갈색	**5** brown	검은색	**14** black
베이지 색	**6** beige	흰색	**15** white
파랑	**7** blue	회색	**16** gray
짙은 남색	**8** navy blue	은색	**17** silver
청록색	**9** turquoise	금색	**18** gold

A. What's your favorite color?
B. **Red**.

A. I like your _____ shirt.
You look very good in _____.

B. Thank you. _____ is my
favorite color.

A. My TV is broken.
B. What's the matter with it?
A. People's faces are _____,
the sky is _____, and the
grass is _____!

Do you know the flags of different countries?
What are the colors of flags you know?

What color makes you happy? What color
makes you sad? Why?

CLOTHING

옷입기

블라우스	1	blouse	캐주얼 상의	11	sport coat / sport jacket/jacket	조끼	20	vest
스커트	2	skirt	정장	12	suit	점퍼 스커트	21	jumper
셔츠	3	shirt	스리피스 정장 (조끼 포함)	13	three-piece suit	블레이저 코트	22	blazer
바지	4	pants/slacks				여성용 쇼트코트	23	tunic
캐주얼 셔츠	5	sport shirt	넥타이	14	tie/necktie	레깅스(보온용 바지)	24	leggings
청바지	6	jeans	단체복	15	uniform	멜빵 바지	25	overalls
니트 셔츠/ 저지 셔츠	7	knit shirt/ jersey	티셔츠	16	T-shirt	터틀넥 스웨터	26	turtleneck
드레스	8	dress	반바지	17	shorts	턱시도	27	tuxedo
스웨터	9	sweater	임부복	18	maternity dress	나비넥타이	28	bow tie
상의/재킷	10	jacket	낙하복	19	jumpsuit	야회복/ 이브닝 드레스	29	(evening) gown

A. I think I'll wear my new **blouse** today.
B. Good idea!

A. I really like your _____.
B. Thank you.
A. Where did you get it/them?
B. At ....

A. Oh, no! I just ripped my _____!
B. What a shame!

What clothing items in this lesson do you wear?

What color clothing do you like to wear?

What do you wear at work or at school? at parties? at weddings?

겉옷

코트	**1**	coat
오버코트/오바	**2**	overcoat
모자(테 있는)	**3**	hat
상의/잠바	**4**	jacket
목도리	**5**	scarf/muffler
스웨터	**6**	sweater jacket
타이츠	**7**	tights
모자	**8**	cap
가죽 재킷	**9**	leather jacket
야구모자	**10**	baseball cap

스포츠용 재킷	**11**	windbreaker
우비 코트	**12**	raincoat
우비 모자	**13**	rain hat
트렌치 코트 (벨트 레인 코트)	**14**	trench coat
우산	**15**	umbrella
판초	**16**	poncho
우비 상의	**17**	rain jacket
장화	**18**	rain boots
스키 모자	**19**	ski hat

스키 잠바	**20**	ski jacket
장갑	**21**	gloves
스키마스크	**22**	ski mask
오리털 잠바	**23**	down jacket
벙어리 장갑	**24**	mittens
파카	**25**	parka
색안경/선글라스	**26**	sunglasses
귀마개/귀덮개	**27**	ear muffs
오리털 조끼	**28**	down vest

A. What's the weather like today?
B. It's cool/cold/raining/snowing.
A. I think I'll wear my _____.

[1–6, 8–17, 19, 20, 22, 23, 25, 28]
A. May I help you?
B. Yes, please. I'm looking for a/an _____.

[7, 18, 21, 24, 26, 27]
A. May I help you?
B. Yes, please. I'm looking for _____.

What do you wear outside when the weather is cool?/when it's raining?/when it's very cold?

잠옷 및 속옷

파자마	**1**	pajamas
나이트 가운	**2**	nightgown
잠옷 (긴 셔츠 모양의)	**3**	nightshirt
목욕 가운	**4**	bathrobe/robe
슬리퍼/실내화	**5**	slippers
담요 잠옷	**6**	blanket sleeper
내의/속셔츠	**7**	undershirt/T-shirt
삼각 팬티	**8**	(jockey) shorts/ underpants/briefs

사각팬티	**9**	boxer shorts/ boxers
국부 보호대/ 급소 보호대	**10**	athletic supporter/ jockstrap
긴 내의	**11**	long underwear/ long johns
양말	**12**	socks
미니 삼각팬티	**13**	(bikini) panties
큰 삼각팬티	**14**	briefs/ underpants

브래지어	**15**	bra
캐미솔 (소매 없는 여자 속옷)	**16**	camisole
반속치마	**17**	half slip
속치마	**18**	(full) slip
스타킹	**19**	stockings
팬티 스타킹	**20**	pantyhose
타이츠	**21**	tights
무릎 양말	**22**	knee-highs
니속스(목이 긴 양말)/ 무릎 양말	**23**	knee socks

A. I can't find my new _____.
B. Did you look in the bureau/dresser/closet?
A. Yes, I did.
B. Then it's/they're probably in the wash.

What sleepwear items do you wear? What sleepwear items do people in your family wear?

운동복과 신발

탱크탑/소매없는 셔츠	**1**	tank top
육상용 반바지/육상복	**2**	running shorts
땀받이 띠	**3**	sweatband
조깅복	**4**	jogging suit/ running suit/ warm-up suit
티셔츠	**5**	T-shirt
스판덱스 반바지	**6**	lycra shorts/ bike shorts
운동복 상의/ 트레이닝복 상의	**7**	sweatshirt
스웨트 팬츠	**8**	sweatpants
수영복 가운	**9**	cover-up

수영복	**10**	swimsuit/ bathing suit
수영 팬츠	**11**	swimming trunks/ swimsuit/ bathing suit
레오타드 (몸에 착 붙는 옷)	**12**	leotard
구두	**13**	shoes
하이힐	**14**	(high) heels
펌프스	**15**	pumps
간편화	**16**	loafers
운동화	**17**	sneakers/ athletic shoes

테니스화/정구화	**18**	tennis shoes
육상화	**19**	running shoes
농구화	**20**	high-tops/ high-top sneakers
샌들	**21**	sandals
고무 슬러퍼	**22**	thongs/ flip-flops
부츠	**23**	boots
작업용 장화	**24**	work boots
등산화	**25**	hiking boots
카우보이 부츠	**26**	cowboy boots
모카신	**27**	moccasins

[1–12]
A. Excuse me. I found this/these _____ in the dryer. Is it/Are they yours?
B. Yes. It's/They're mine. Thank you.

[13–27]
A. Are those new _____?
B. Yes, they are.
A. They're very nice.
B. Thanks.

Do you exercise? What do you do? What kind of clothing do you wear when you exercise?

What kind of shoes do you wear when you go to work or to school? when you exercise? when you relax at home? when you go out with friends or family members?

보석 및 장식품

반지	**1**	ring
약혼반지	**2**	engagement ring
결혼반지	**3**	wedding ring/wedding band
귀걸이	**4**	earrings
목걸이	**5**	necklace
진주목걸이	**6**	pearl necklace/pearls/ string of pearls
목걸이/목걸이 줄	**7**	chain
구슬목걸이	**8**	beads
장식핀/브로치	**9**	pin/brooch
로켓(목걸이에 다는 금속 곽)	**10**	locket
팔찌	**11**	bracelet
머리핀	**12**	barrette
커프스 단추/소맷부리 단추	**13**	cuff links
멜빵	**14**	suspenders
손목시계	**15**	watch/wrist watch
손수건	**16**	handkerchief
열쇠고리	**17**	key ring/key chain
동전지갑	**18**	change purse
지갑	**19**	wallet
벨트/허리띠	**20**	belt
핸드백	**21**	purse/handbag/pocketbook
어깨가방	**22**	shoulder bag
토트백(여성용 대형 손가방)	**23**	tote bag
책가방	**24**	book bag
배낭	**25**	backpack
화장가방	**26**	makeup bag
서류가방	**27**	briefcase

A. Oh, no! I think I lost my **ring**!
B. I'll help you look for it.

A. Oh, no! I think I lost my **earrings**!
B. I'll help you look for them.

[In a store]
A. Excuse me. Is this/Are these _____ on sale this week?
B. Yes. It's/They're half price.

[On the street]
A. Help! Police! Stop that man/woman!
B. What happened?!
A. He/She just stole my _____ and my _____!

Do you like to wear jewelry? What jewelry do you have?

In your country, what do men, women, and children use to carry their things?

의복 묘사하기

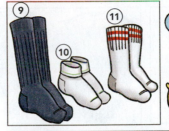

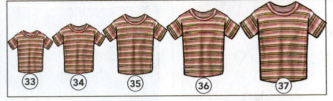

옷의 종류	**Types of Clothing**		면 플란넬 셔츠	**19** flannel *shirt*
긴팔 셔츠	**1** long-sleeved shirt		폴리에스테르 블라우스	**20** polyester *blouse*
반팔 셔츠	**2** short-sleeved shirt		린넨 드레스	**21** linen *dress*
소매없는 셔츠	**3** sleeveless shirt		비단 스카프	**22** silk *scarf*
터틀넥 셔츠	**4** turtleneck (shirt)		양모 스웨터	**23** wool *sweater*
브이넥 스웨터	**5** V-neck sweater		밀집 모자	**24** straw *hat*
카디건	**6** cardigan sweater		무늬	**Patterns**
크루넥 스웨터(깃없는 스웨터)	**7** crewneck sweater		줄무늬의	**25** striped
터틀넥 스웨터	**8** turtleneck sweater		바둑판 무늬의	**26** checked
무릎 양말	**9** knee-high socks		격자무늬의/체크무늬의	**27** plaid
발목 양말	**10** ankle socks		물방울 무늬의	**28** polka-dotted
크루삭(골이 진 두꺼운 양말)	**11** crew socks		무늬가 있는	**29** patterned/print
(뚫은 귀용) 귀걸이	**12** pierced earrings		꽃무늬의	**30** flowered/floral
클립 고정식 귀걸이	**13** clip-on earrings		페이즐리 무늬의	**31** paisley
재질 종류	**Types of Material**		파랑 단색의	**32** solid *blue*
코르덴 바지	**14** corduroy *pants*		크기	**Sizes**
가죽 부츠	**15** leather *boots*		특소의	**33** extra-small
나이론 스타킹	**16** nylon *stockings*		소형	**34** small
면 티셔츠	**17** cotton *T-shirt*		중간 크기의	**35** medium
데님 재킷	**18** denim *jacket*		대형	**36** large
			특대형	**37** extra-large

[1–24]
A. May I help you?
B. Yes, please. I'm looking for a *shirt*.*
A. What kind?
B. I'm looking for a *long-sleeved shirt*.

* With 9–16: I'm looking for _____.

[25–32]
A. How do you like this _____ tie/shirt/skirt?
B. Actually, I prefer that _____ one.

[33–37]
A. What size are you looking for?
B. _____.

Describe your favorite clothing items. For each item, tell about the color, the type of material, the size, and the pattern.

옷 문제점들과 수선

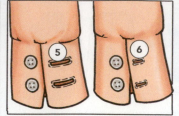

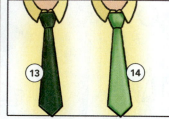
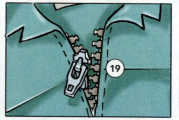

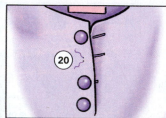

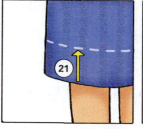

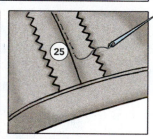

긴-짧은	**1–2** long – short	얼룩진 깃(칼라)	**17** stained *collar*
꽉 끼는-헐거운	**3–4** tight – loose/baggy	트더진 주머니	**18** ripped/torn *pocket*
큰-작은	**5–6** large/big – small	고장 난 지퍼	**19** broken *zipper*
높은-낮은	**7–8** high – low	떨어져 없어진 단추	**20** missing *button*
화려한-평범한	**9–10** fancy – plain	스커트 길이를 줄이다	**21** shorten the *skirt*
무거운-가벼운	**11–12** heavy – light	소매를 늘이다	**22** lengthen the *sleeves*
진한-엷은/옅은	**13–14** dark – light	재킷 품을 줄이다	**23** take in the *jacket*
넓은-좁은	**15–16** wide – narrow	바지를 늘이다	**24** let out the *pants*
		솔기를 고치다/손질하다	**25** fix/repair the *seam*

[1–2]
A. Are the sleeves too **long**?
B. No. They're too **short**.

1–2	Are the sleeves too _____?	9–10	Are the buttons too _____?
3–4	Are the pants too _____?	11–12	Is the coat too _____?
5–6	Are the buttonholes too _____?	13–14	Is the color too _____?
7–8	Are the heels too _____?	15–16	Are the lapels too _____?

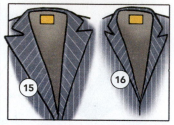

[17–20]
A. What's the matter with it?
B. It has a **stained** *collar*.

[21–25]
A. Please **shorten** the *skirt*.
B. **Shorten** the *skirt*? Okay.

Tell about the differences between clothing people wear now and clothing people wore a long time ago.

세탁물

세탁물을 분류하다	**A** sort the laundry		표백제	**9** bleach	
세탁기에 옷을 넣다	**B** load the washer		젖은 옷	**10** wet clothing	
세탁기에서 옷을 꺼내다	**C** unload the washer		빨래 건조기	**11** dryer	
건조기에 옷을 넣다	**D** load the dryer		보플 트랩	**12** lint trap	
빨래줄에 옷을 걸다	**E** hang clothes on the clothesline		정전기 제거제	**13** static cling remover	
다리미	**F** iron		빨랫줄	**14** clothesline	
세탁물을 접다	**G** fold the laundry		빨래집게	**15** clothespin	
옷을 걸다	**H** hang up clothing		다리미	**16** iron	
물건을 정리해 넣어놓다	**I** put things away		다림질 판	**17** ironing board	
			주름진 옷	**18** wrinkled clothing	
세탁물	**1** laundry		다려진 옷	**19** ironed clothing	
밝은 색 의류	**2** light clothing		녹말 분무기	**20** spray starch	
어두운 색 의류	**3** dark clothing		세탁된 옷	**21** clean clothing	
빨래 바구니	**4** laundry basket		벽장	**22** closet	
빨래 자루	**5** laundry bag		옷걸이	**23** hanger	
세탁기	**6** washer/washing machine		서랍	**24** drawer	
세탁세제	**7** laundry detergent		선반	**25** shelf-shelves	
섬유 유연제	**8** fabric softener				

[A–I]
A. What are you doing?
B. I'm _____ing.

[4–6, 11, 14–17, 23]
A. Excuse me. Do you sell _____s?
B. Yes. They're at the back of the store.
A. Thank you.

[7–9, 13, 20]
A. Excuse me. Do you sell _____?
B. Yes. It's at the back of the store.
A. Thank you.

Who does the laundry in your home? What things does this person use?

백화점

(매장) 안내판	**1**	(store) directory	
귀금속카운터	**2**	Jewelry Counter	
향수카운터	**3**	Perfume Counter	
에스컬레이터	**4**	escalator	
엘리베이터/승강기	**5**	elevator	
남성의류매장	**6**	Men's Clothing Department	
고객인수처	**7**	customer pickup area	
여성의류매장	**8**	Women's Clothing Department	
아동의류매장	**9**	Children's Clothing Department	

주방기구매장	**10**	Housewares Department
가구매장	**11**	Furniture Department/ Home Furnishings Department
가전제품매장	**12**	Household Appliances Department
전자제품매장	**13**	Electronics Department
고객서비스카운터	**14**	Customer Assistance Counter/ Customer Service Counter
신사용 화장실	**15**	men's room
숙녀용 화장실	**16**	ladies' room
식수대	**17**	water fountain
간이식당/매점/스낵코너	**18**	snack bar
선물포장카운터	**19**	Gift Wrap Counter

A. Excuse me. Where's the **store directory**?
B. It's over there, next to the **Jewelry Counter**.
A. Thanks.
B. You're welcome.

A. Excuse me. Do you sell *ties**?
B. Yes. You can find *ties** in the ____[6, 8–13]____ /at the ____[2, 3]____ on the first/second/third/fourth floor.
A. Thank you.

**ties/bracelets/dresses/toasters/. . .*

Describe a department store you know. Tell what is on each floor.

쇼핑

사다	**A** buy	판매 팻말	**1** sale sign	관리 주의사항	**8** care instructions
반품하다	**B** return	상품 레벨	**2** label	정가	**9** regular price
교환하다	**C** exchange	가격표	**3** price tag	특매가격/	**10** sale price
입어보다	**D** try on	영수증	**4** receipt	세일가격	
값을 지불하다	**E** pay for	할인	**5** discount	가격	**11** price
~에 관한 정보를 얻다	**F** get some information about	크기/사이즈	**6** size	판매세	**12** sales tax
		소재	**7** material	총가격	**13** total price

A. May I help you?
B. Yes, please. I want to ___[A–F]___ this item.
A. Certainly. I'll be glad to help you.

A. { What's the ___[5–7, 9–13]___?
{ What are the ___[8]___?
B. _____.
A. Are you sure?
B. Yes. Look at the ___[1–4]___!

Which stores in your area have sales? How often?

Tell about something you bought on sale.

비디오와 오디오 장비

텔레비전	**1**	TV/television
플라스마 텔레비전	**2**	plasma TV
액정 텔레비전	**3**	LCD TV
투사선 텔레비전	**4**	projection TV
휴대용 텔레비전	**5**	portable TV
리모컨	**6**	remote (control)
디비디	**7**	DVD
디비디 재생기	**8**	DVD player
비디오 테이프	**9**	video/videocassette/ videotape
비디오 카세트 녹화기	**10**	VCR/videocassette recorder
캠코더/비디오 카메라	**11**	camcorder/video camera
배터리 팩	**12**	battery pack
배터리 충전기	**13**	battery charger
라디오	**14**	radio
라디오 시계	**15**	clock radio
단파 라디오	**16**	shortwave radio
녹음기	**17**	tape recorder/cassette recorder
마이크	**18**	microphone

스테레오 시스템	**19**	stereo system/sound system
레코드	**20**	record
턴테이블	**21**	turntable
시디/콤팩트 디스크	**22**	CD/compact disc
CD재생기	**23**	CD player
튜너	**24**	tuner
카세트 테이프	**25**	(audio)tape/(audio)cassette
테이프 데크	**26**	tape deck/cassette deck
스피커	**27**	speakers
휴대용 스테레오	**28**	portable stereo system/ boombox
휴대용CD재생기	**29**	portable/personal CD player
휴대용카세트재생기	**30**	portable/personal cassette player
헤드폰	**31**	headphones
휴대용디지털오디오재생기	**32**	portable/personal digital audio player
비디오게임 기구	**33**	video game system
비디오게임	**34**	video game
휴대용 비디오게임기	**35**	hand-held video game

A. May I help you?
B. Yes, please. I'm looking for a **TV**.

With 27 & 31, use: I'm looking for _____.

A. I like your new _____.
 Where did you get it/them?
B. At …..*(name of store)*…

A. Which company makes the best
 _____?
B. In my opinion, the best _____
 is/are made by …………..

What video and audio equipment do you have or want?

In your opinion, which brands of video and audio equipment are the best?

전화와 카메라

전화	1	telephone/phone
무선 전화기	2	cordless phone
휴대폰	3	cell phone/cellular phone
배터리	4	battery
배터리 충전기	5	battery charger
자동응답기	6	answering machine
휴대용 무선호출기	7	pager
피디에이 (개인 휴대용 정보 단말기)	8	PDA/electronic personal organizer
팩스	9	fax machine
휴대용 전자계산기	10	(pocket) calculator
계산기	11	adding machine
전압 조정기	12	voltage regulator
어댑터	13	adapter
35미리 카메라	14	(35 millimeter) camera
렌즈	15	lens
필름	16	film
줌렌즈	17	zoom lens
디지털 카메라	18	digital camera
메모리 디스크	19	memory disk
삼각대	20	tripod
플래시	21	flash (attachment)
카메라 가방	22	camera case
환등기	23	slide projector
영사막	24	(movie) screen

A. Can I help you?
B. Yes. I want to buy a **telephone**.*

* With 16, use: I want to buy _____.

A. Excuse me. Do you sell _____s?*
B. Yes. We have a large selection of _____s.

* With 16, use the singular.

A. Which _____ is the best?
B. This one here. It's made by _____(company)_____.

What kind of telephone do you use?

Do you have a camera? What kind is it?
What do you take pictures of?

Does anyone you know have an answering machine?
When you call, what message do you hear?

컴퓨터

Computer Hardware   컴퓨터 하드웨어

데스크탑 컴퓨터	1	(desktop) computer
중앙처리장치	2	CPU/central processing unit
모니터/화면	3	monitor/screen
시디롬 드라이브	4	CD-ROM drive
시디롬	5	CD-ROM
디스크 드라이브	6	disk drive
디스크	7	(floppy) disk
자판/키보드	8	keyboard
마우스	9	mouse
평면 모니터	10	flat panel screen/ LCD screen
노트북 컴퓨터	11	notebook computer
조종간(게임의)	12	joystick
트랙볼	13	track ball
모뎀	14	modem
전압안전장치	15	surge protector
프린터	16	printer
스캐너	17	scanner
케이블	18	cable

Computer Software   컴퓨터 소프트웨어

워드 프로세싱 프로그램	19	word-processing program
스프레드시트 프로그램	20	spreadsheet program
교육용 소프트웨어	21	educational software program
컴퓨터게임	22	computer game

A. Can you recommend a good **computer**?
B. Yes. This **computer** here is excellent.

A. Is that a new _____?
B. Yes.
A. Where did you get it?
B. At ......*(name of store)*......

A. May I help you?
B. Yes, please. Do you sell _____s?
A. Yes. We carry a complete line of _____s.

Do you use a computer? When?

In your opinion, how have computers changed the world?

보드게임	**1** board game
조각 그림 맞추기/퍼즐	**2** (jigsaw) puzzle
공작세트	**3** construction set
블록(완구의)	**4** (building) blocks
고무공	**5** rubber ball
비치볼	**6** beach ball
모래삽 달린 양동이	**7** pail and shovel
인형	**8** doll
인형옷	**9** doll clothing
인형집	**10** doll house
인형집 가구	**11** doll house furniture
전투 인형	**12** action figure
헝겊 동물인형	**13** stuffed animal

미니카/장난감 차	**14** matchbox car
장난감 트럭	**15** toy truck
경주용 자동차세트	**16** racing car set
장난감 기차세트	**17** train set
모형조립세트	**18** model kit
과학실험세트	**19** science kit
워키토키	**20** walkie-talkie (set)
훌라후프	**21** hula hoop
줄넘기 줄	**22** jump rope
비누방울액	**23** bubble soap
트레이딩 카드	**24** trading cards
크레용	**25** crayons
칼라 마커펜/ 칼라 사인펜	**26** (color) markers

색칠하기 그림책	**27** coloring book
색도화지	**28** construction paper
물감세트	**29** paint set
찰흙	**30** (modeling) clay
스티커	**31** stickers
자전거	**32** bicycle
세발자전거	**33** tricycle
수레	**34** wagon
스케이트 보드	**35** skateboard
장난감 그네세트	**36** swing set
장난감 집	**37** play house
튜브 풀	**38** kiddie pool/ inflatable pool

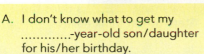

A. Excuse me. I'm looking for (a/an) _____(s) for my *grandson*.*
B. Look in the next aisle.
A. Thank you.

* *grandson/granddaughter/. . .*

A. I don't know what to get my
   ....-year-old son/daughter
   for his/her birthday.
B. What about (a) _____?
A. Good idea! Thanks.

A. Mom/Dad? Can we buy
   this/these _____?
B. No, *Johnny*. Not today.

What toys are most popular in your country?

What were your favorite toys when you were a child?

입금하다	**A** make a deposit	여행자수표	**4** traveler's check
출금하다	**B** make a withdrawal	은행통장	**5** bankbook/passbook
수표를 현금화하다	**C** cash a check	자동 현금카드/현금카드	**6** ATM card
여행자수표를 받다	**D** get traveler's checks	신용카드	**7** credit card
계좌를 개설하다	**E** open an account	금고	**8** (bank) vault
대부를 신청하다	**F** apply for a loan	귀중품 보관함/대여금고	**9** safe deposit box
환전하다	**G** exchange currency	은행출납원	**10** teller
		경비원/청원 경찰	**11** security guard
입금용지	**1** deposit slip	현금자동입출금기	**12** ATM (machine)/ cash machine
인출용지/예금청구서	**2** withdrawal slip		
수표	**3** check	은행원	**13** bank officer

[A–G]
A. Where are you going?
B. I'm going to the bank.
   I have to _____ .

[5–7]
A. What are you looking for?
B. My _____ . I can't find it
   anywhere!

[8–13]
A. How many _____ s does the
   State Street Bank have?
B. ....

Do you have a bank account? What kind?
Where? What do you do at the bank?

Do you ever use traveler's checks?
When?

Do you have a credit card?
What kind? When do you use it?

재정

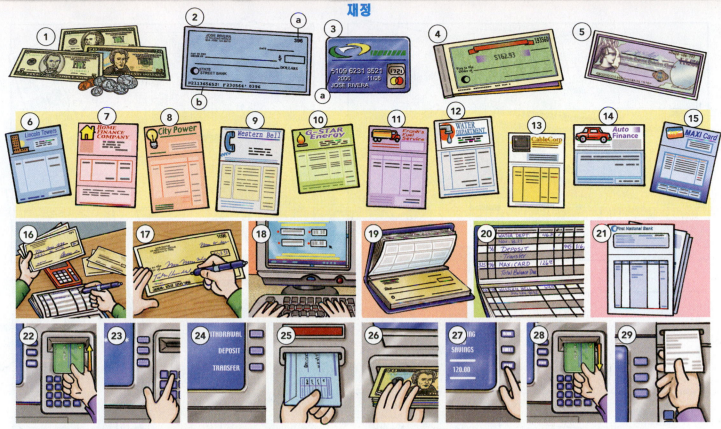

지불 형태 / Forms of Payment

현금	1	cash
수표	2	check
수표 번호	a	check number
계좌 번호	b	account number
신용카드	3	credit card
신용카드번호	a	credit card number
우편환	4	money order
여행자 수표	5	traveler's check

가계 청구서 / Household Bills

임대료	6	rent
주택융자 상환금	7	mortgage payment
전기요금 청구서	8	electric bill
전화요금청구서	9	telephone bill
가스요금 청구서	10	gas bill
연료비 청구서	11	oil bill/heating bill
수도요금 청구서	12	water bill
케이블 텔레비전 청구서	13	cable TV bill
자동차 지불	14	car payment
신용카드 청구서	15	credit card bill

가계 재정 / Family Finances

수표장부를 결산하다	16	balance the checkbook
수표를 발행하다	17	write a check
온라인 은행	18	bank online
수표책	19	checkbook
수표 장부	20	check register
월별 거래 내역서	21	monthly statement

현금자동입출금기 이용하기 / Using an ATM Machine

현금자동입출금카드를 넣다	22	insert the ATM card
개인 비밀번호를 입력하다	23	enter your PIN number/ personal identification number
거래 종류를 선택하다	24	select a transaction
현금을 입금하다	25	make a deposit
현금을 인출하다	26	withdraw/get cash
예금액을 이체하다	27	transfer funds
카드를 빼다	28	remove your card
거래 전표를 받다/영수증 받다	29	take your transaction slip/receipt

A. Can I pay by ___[1, 2]___ / with a ___[3-5]___ ?
B. Yes. We accept ___[1]___ / ___[2-5]___ s.

A. What are you doing?
B. I'm paying the ___[6-15]___.
   I'm ___[16-18]___ ing.
   I'm looking for the ___[19-21]___.

A. What should I do?
B. ___[22-29]___.

What household bills do you receive?
How much do you pay for the different bills?

Who takes care of the finances in your household? What does that person do?

Do you use ATM machines?
If you do, how do you use them?

우체국

편지	1	letter	우표 1롤	12	roll of stamps	우편번호	21	zip code
엽서	2	postcard	우표 1권	13	book of stamps	소인	22	postmark
항공우편	3	air letter/ aerogramme	우편환	14	money order	우표	23	stamp/ postage
소포	4	package/parcel	주소변경통지서	15	change-of-address form	우편함 입구	24	mail slot
1종우편	5	first class	특별 등기 우편 신청서	16	selective service registration form	우체국 직원	25	postal worker/ postal clerk
특급 우편물	6	priority mail	여권 신청 양식	17	passport application form	저울	26	scale
속달우편	7	express mail/ overnight mail				우표 자동판매기	27	stamp machine
소포우편	8	parcel post	봉투	18	envelope	우편집배원	28	letter carrier/ mail carrier
배달증명우편	9	certified mail	발신인 주소	19	return address	우편 트럭	29	mail truck
우표	10	stamp	우편 주소	20	mailing address	우체통	30	mailbox
우표 전지 한 장	11	sheet of stamps						

[1–4]
A. Where are you going?
B. To the post office. I have to mail a/an _____ .

[5–9]
A. How do you want to send it?
B. _____ , please.

[10–17]
A. Next!
B. I'd like a _____ , please.
A. Here you are.

[19–21, 23]
A. Do you want me to mail this letter?
B. Yes, thanks.
A. Oops! You forgot the _____ !

How often do you go to the post office? What do you do there?

Tell about the postal system in your country.

도서관

온라인 도서목록	1 online catalog	신문	13 newspapers	마이크로 필름	24 microfilm
도서목록카드	2 card catalog	미디어 코너	14 media section	마이크로 필름	25 microfilm
저자	3 author	오디오북	15 books on tape	투영장치	reader
도서명	4 title	오디오테이프	16 audiotapes	사전	26 dictionary
도서대출증	5 library card	시디	17 CDs	백과사전	27 encyclopedia
복사기	6 copier/	비디오 테이프	18 videotapes	지도책	28 atlas
	photocopier/	컴퓨터	19 (computer)	참고자료 데스크	29 reference desk
	copy machine	소프트웨어	software	참고자료 사서	30 (reference)
책장	7 shelves	디비디	20 DVDs		librarian
어린이 코너	8 children's section	외서 코너	21 foreign language	대여 데스크	31 checkout desk
아동도서	9 children's books		section	도서관 직원	32 library clerk
정기간행물 코너	10 periodical section	외서	22 foreign language		
저널	11 journals		books		
잡지	12 magazines	참고자료실	23 reference section		

[1, 2, 6–32]
A. Excuse me. Where's/Where are the _____?
B. Over there, at/near/next to the _____.

[8–23, 26–28]
A. Excuse me. Where can I find a/an __[26–28]__ / __[9, 11–13, 15–20, 22]__?
B. Look in the __[8, 10, 14, 21, 23]__ over there.

A. I'm having trouble finding a book.
B. Do you know the __[3–4]__?
A. Yes. ………….

A. Excuse me. I'd like to check out this __[26–28]__/these __[11–13]__.
B. I'm sorry. It/They must remain in the library.

Do you go to a library? Where?
What does this library have?

Tell about how you use the library.

지역사회 기관

경찰서 **A** police station		소방수 **5** firefighter
소방서 **B** fire station		응급실 **6** emergency room
병원 **C** hospital		응급구조대원 **7** EMT/paramedic
시청 **D** town hall/city hall		구급차 **8** ambulance
레크레이션 센터 **E** recreation center		시장 **9** mayor/city manager
쓰레기장 **F** dump		회의실 **10** meeting room
탁아소/놀이방 **G** child-care center		체육관 **11** gym
양로원 **H** senior center		여가 활동 지도자 **12** activities director
교회 **I** church		오락실 **13** game room
유대 교회 **J** synagogue		수영장 **14** swimming pool
모스크 (이슬람교 성원) **K** mosque		환경 미화원 **15** sanitation worker
사원 **L** temple		재활용 센터 **16** recycling center
		보육사 **17** child-care worker
응급전화 교환원 **1** emergency operator		탁아소 **18** nursery
경찰 **2** police officer		놀이방 **19** playroom
경찰차 **3** police car		양로원 직원 **20** eldercare worker/
소방차 **4** fire engine		senior care worker

[A–L]
A. Where are you going?
B. I'm going to the _____.

[1, 2, 5, 7, 12, 15, 17, 20]
A. What do you do?
B. I'm a/an _____.

[3, 4, 8]
A. Do you hear a siren?
B. Yes. There's a/an _____ coming up behind us.

What community institutions are in your city or town? Where are they located?

Which community institutions do you use? When?

Korean	#	English	Korean	#	English	Korean	#	English
자동차 사고	1	car accident	차량 강탈	9	car jacking	절단된 전선	16	downed power line
화재	2	fire	은행강도질	10	bank robbery	화학약품유출	17	chemical spill
폭발	3	explosion	폭행	11	assault	기차 탈선	18	train derailment
강도질	4	robbery	살인	12	murder	공공시설물 파괴	19	vandalism
도둑질	5	burglary	정전	13	blackout/ power outage	갱 폭력	20	gang violence
폭력강도	6	mugging	가스 누출	14	gas leak	음주 운전	21	drunk driving
유괴	7	kidnapping	급수 본관 파열	15	water main break	마약 거래	22	drug dealing
미아	8	lost child						

[1–13]
A. I want to report a/an _____.
B. What's your location?
A. ....

[14–18]
A. Why is this street closed?
B. It's closed because of a _____.

[19–22]
A. I'm very concerned about the amount of _____ in our community.
B. I agree. _____ is a very serious problem.

Is there much crime in your community? Tell about it.

Have you ever experienced a crime or emergency? What happened?

몸

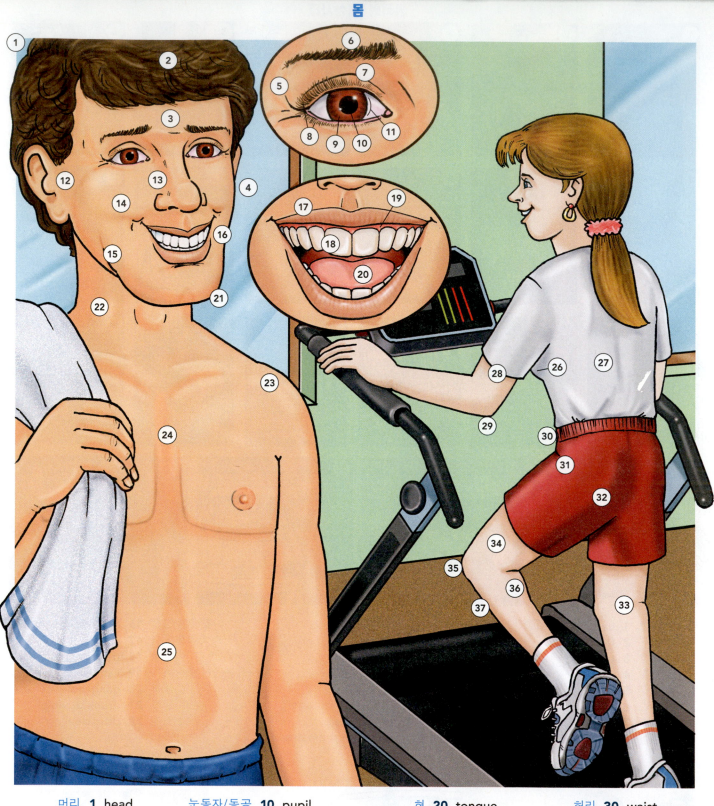

머리	1	head
머리카락/ 모발/머리	2	hair
이마	3	forehead
얼굴	4	face
눈	5	eye
눈썹	6	eyebrow
눈꺼풀	7	eyelid
속눈썹	8	eyelashes
홍채	9	iris

눈동자/동공	10	pupil
각막	11	cornea
귀	12	ear
코	13	nose
볼/뺨	14	cheek
턱	15	jaw
입	16	mouth
입술	17	lip
치아	18	tooth–teeth
잇몸	19	gums

혀	20	tongue
아래 턱/턱 끝	21	chin
목	22	neck
어깨	23	shoulder
가슴	24	chest
복부	25	abdomen
유방	26	breast
등	27	back
팔	28	arm
팔꿈치	29	elbow

허리	30	waist
둔부/히프	31	hip
엉덩이	32	buttocks
다리	33	leg
허벅지	34	thigh
무릎	35	knee
종아리	36	calf
정강이	37	shin

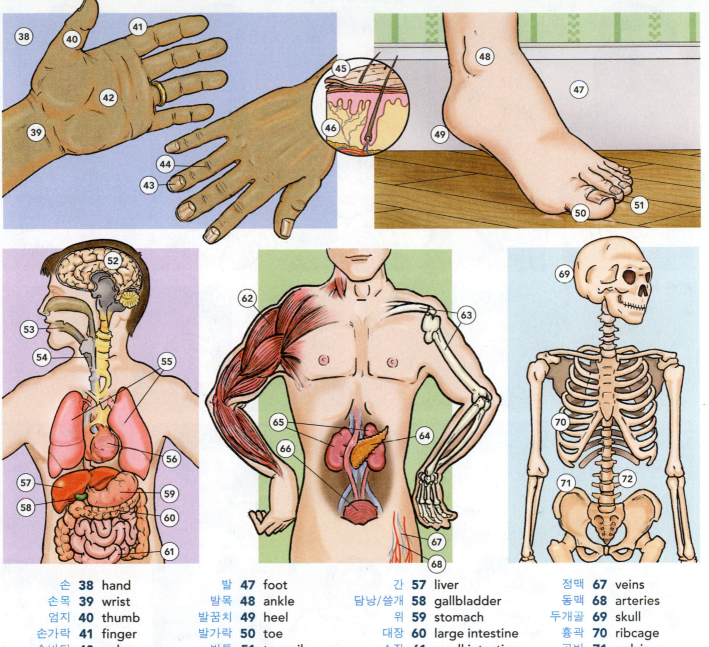

손	**38** hand	발	**47** foot	간	**57** liver
손목	**39** wrist	발목	**48** ankle	담낭/쓸개	**58** gallbladder
엄지	**40** thumb	발꿈치	**49** heel	위	**59** stomach
손가락	**41** finger	발가락	**50** toe	대장	**60** large intestine
손바닥	**42** palm	발톱	**51** toenail	소장	**61** small intestine
손톱	**43** fingernail	뇌	**52** brain	근육	**62** muscles
손가락 관절/ 손가락 마디	**44** knuckle	목(구멍)	**53** throat	뼈	**63** bones
피부	**45** skin	식도	**54** esophagus	췌장	**64** pancreas
신경	**46** nerve	폐	**55** lungs	신장	**65** kidneys
		심장	**56** heart	방광	**66** bladder

정맥	**67** veins
동맥	**68** arteries
두개골	**69** skull
흉곽	**70** ribcage
골반	**71** pelvis
척추	**72** spinal column/ spinal cord

A. My doctor checked my **head** and said everything is okay.
B. I'm glad to hear that.

[1, 3–7, 12–29, 31–51]

A. Ooh!
B. What's the matter?
   My _____ hurts!
   My _____ s hurt!

[52–72]

A. My doctor wants me to have some tests.
B. Why?
A. She's concerned about my _____.

Describe yourself as completely as you can.

Which parts of the body are most important at school? at work? when you play your favorite sport?

질병, 증상 및 상처

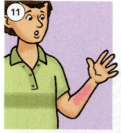     

 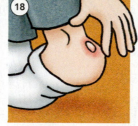 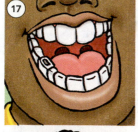  

두통	**1** headache	염증/감염	**10** infection
귀앓이/이통	**2** earache	발진/두드러기	**11** rash
치통	**3** toothache	벌레물린 상처	**12** insect bite
복통	**4** stomachache	햇볕에 탐	**13** sunburn
요통	**5** backache	목이 뻐근함	**14** stiff neck
인후염/목감기	**6** sore throat	콧물	**15** runny nose
열	**7** fever/temperature	코피	**16** bloody nose
감기	**8** cold	충치	**17** cavity
기침	**9** cough	수포	**18** blister

사마귀	**19** wart
딸꾹질	**20** (the) hiccups
오한	**21** (the) chills
경련	**22** cramps
설사	**23** diarrhea
흉부통	**24** chest pain
호흡곤란	**25** shortness of breath
후두염	**26** laryngitis

A. What's the matter?
B. I have a/an _____[1–19]_____.

A. What's the matter?
B. I have _____[20–26]_____.

기절할 것 같은	27	faint	지친	32	exhausted	출혈하다	38	bleed	다치다	44	hurt–hurt
어지러운	28	dizzy	기침하다	33	cough	꼬이다	39	twist	벤	45	cut–cut
메스꺼운	29	nauseous	재채기하다	34	sneeze	할퀴다	40	scratch	삐다	46	sprain
부은	30	bloated	씨근거리다 (천식으로)	35	wheeze	스쳐 상처를 내다	41	scrape	탈구시키다	47	dislocate
충혈된/ 코가 막힌	31	congested	트림하다	36	burp	타박상을 입다	42	bruise	부러진	48	break–broke
			구토하다	37	vomit/ throw up	화상을 입다	43	burn	부은	49	swollen
									가려운	50	itchy

A. What's the problem?
B. { I feel [27–30] .
     I'm [31–32] .
     I've been [33–38] ing a lot.

A. What happened?
B. { I [39–45] ed my ....
     I think I [46–48] ed my ....
     My .... is/are [49–50] .

A. How do you feel?
B. Not so good./Not very well./Terrible!
A. What's the matter?
B. ...., ..., and ....
A. I'm sorry to hear that.

Tell about the last time you didn't feel well. What was the matter?

Tell about a time you hurt yourself. What happened? How? What did you do about it?

What do you do when you have a cold? a stomachache? an insect bite? the hiccups?

구급

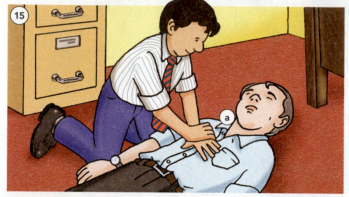

응급조치 교본	**1** first-aid manual	아스피린	**13** aspirin
구급상자	**2** first-aid kit	비아스피린 진통제	**14** non-aspirin pain reliever
가제 붙은 반창고	**3** (adhesive) bandage/ Band-Aid™	심폐기능소생법	**15** CPR (cardiopulmonary resuscitation)
살균세척지	**4** antiseptic cleansing wipe	맥박이 없다	**a** has no pulse
살균붕대	**5** sterile (dressing) pad	인공호흡	**16** rescue breathing
과산화 수소	**6** hydrogen peroxide	숨을 쉬지 않는다	**b** isn't breathing
항생제 연고	**7** antibiotic ointment	하임리크 구명법	**17** the Heimlich maneuver
가제	**8** gauze	숨이 막혀 있다	**c** is choking
반창고	**9** adhesive tape	부목	**18** splint
족집게	**10** tweezers	손가락이 부러졌다	**d** broke a finger
항히스타민제 크림	**11** antihistamine cream	지혈대	**19** tourniquet
붕대/탄력 붕대	**12** elastic bandage/ Ace™ bandage	피를 흘리다	**e** is bleeding

A. Do we have any ____[3–5, 12]____s/
____[6–11, 13, 14]____?
B. Yes. Look in the first-aid kit.

A. Help! My friend ____[a–e]____!
B. I can help!
{ I know how to do ____[15–17]____.
{ I can make a ____[18, 19]____.

Do you have a first-aid kit? If you do, what's in it? If you don't, where can you buy one?

Tell about a time when you gave or received first aid.

Where can a person learn first aid in your community?

의료 비상사태 및 병

다친	**1** hurt/injured	패혈성 인두염	**14** strep throat
쇼크를 받은	**2** in shock	홍역	**15** measles
의식 불명의	**3** unconscious	유행성 이하선염	**16** mumps
일사병	**4** heatstroke	수두	**17** chicken pox
동상	**5** frostbite	천식	**18** asthma
심장발작	**6** heart attack	암	**19** cancer
알레르기 반응	**7** allergic reaction	우울증	**20** depression
독극물을 마시다	**8** swallow poison	당뇨병	**21** diabetes
약물을 과량 복용하다	**9** overdose on drugs	심장병	**22** heart disease
넘어지다	**10** fall–fell	고혈압	**23** high blood pressure/ hypertension
감전이 되다	**11** get–got an electric shock	폐결핵	**24** TB/tuberculosis
독감	**12** the flu/influenza	에이즈	**25** AIDS*
이염	**13** an ear infection		* Acquired Immune Deficiency Syndrome

A. What happened?

B. My ....
{
is ___[1–3]___.
has ___[4–5]___.
is having a/an ___[6–7]___.
___[8–11]___ed.
}

A. What's your location?

B. ....(address)..................

A. My .... is sick.

B. What's the matter?

A. He/She has ___[12–25]___.

B. I'm sorry to hear that.

Tell about a medical emergency that happened to you or someone you know.

Which illnesses in this lesson are you familiar with?

의료 검사

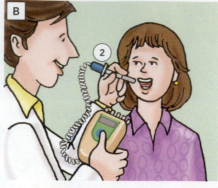

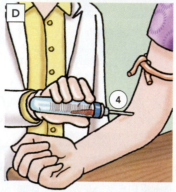

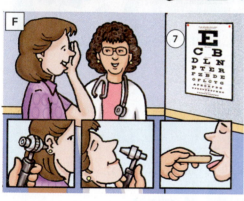

키와 몸무게를 재다	**A**	measure *your* height and weight
체온을 재다	**B**	take *your* temperature
혈압을 재다	**C**	check *your* blood pressure
피를 뽑다	**D**	draw some blood
건강에 대하여 몇 가지 질문을 하다	**E**	ask *you* some questions about *your* health
눈, 귀, 코를 검사하다	**F**	examine *your* eyes, ears, nose, and throat
심장 소리를 듣다	**G**	listen to *your* heart
흉곽 X 레이를 찍다	**H**	take a chest X-ray

체중계	**1**	scale
체온계	**2**	thermometer
혈압계	**3**	blood pressure gauge
주사	**4**	needle/syringe
진찰실	**5**	examination room
진료대	**6**	examination table
시력검사표	**7**	eye chart
청진기	**8**	stethoscope
엑스레이기	**9**	X-ray machine

[A–H]
A. Now I'm going to **measure your height and weight**.
B. All right.

[A–H]
A. What did the doctor/nurse do during the examination?
B. She/He **measured my height and weight**.

[1–3, 5–9]
A. So, how do you like our new **scale?**
B. It's very nice, doctor.

How often do you have a medical exam? What does the doctor/nurse do?

의료 및 치과 절차들

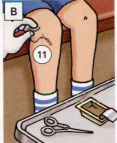

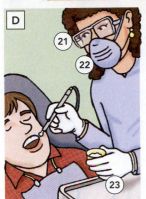

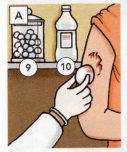

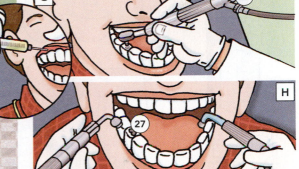

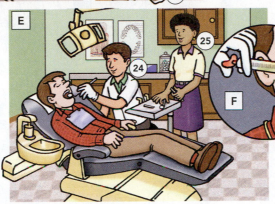

상처를 세정하다	**A** clean the wound	의료기록서	**4** medical history form	얼음 주머니	**16** ice pack
상처를 봉합하다	**B** close the wound	진찰실	**5** examination room	처방(전)	**17** prescription
상처를 감싸다	**C** dress the wound	의사/내과의사	**6** doctor/physician	삼각건	**18** sling
이를 세정하다	**D** clean *your* teeth	환자	**7** patient	깁스 붕대	**19** cast
이를 검사하다	**E** examine *your* teeth	간호사	**8** nurse	부목	**20** brace
마취 주사를 놓다	**F** give *you* a shot of anesthetic/ Novocaine™	탈지면	**9** cotton balls	치과 위생사	**21** dental hygienist
		알코올	**10** alcohol	마스크	**22** mask
충치구멍을 뚫다	**G** drill the cavity	봉합	**11** stitches	장갑	**23** gloves
이를 메우다	**H** fill the tooth	가제	**12** gauze	치과의사	**24** dentist
		테이프	**13** tape	치과보조원	**25** dental assistant
대기실	**1** waiting room	주사	**14** injection/shot	뚫다	**26** drill
안내원	**2** receptionist	목발	**15** crutches	메움	**27** filling
보험카드	**3** insurance card				

A. Now I'm going to { _____ [A–H]. give you (a/an) _____ [14–17]. put your .... in a _____ [18–20]. }

B. Okay.

A. I need { _____ [9, 10, 12, 13, 23]. a _____ [22, 26]. }

B. Here you are.

Tell about a personal experience you had with a medical or dental procedure.

의학적 진단

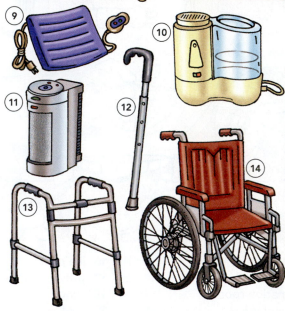

침대에서 휴식을 취하다/쉬다	**1** rest in bed	공기 청정기	**11** air purifier
수분을 섭취하다	**2** drink fluids	지팡이	**12** cane
양치질하다	**3** gargle	보행 보조기	**13** walker
식이요법을 하다	**4** go on a diet	휠체어	**14** wheelchair
운동하다	**5** exercise	혈액검사	**15** blood work/blood tests
비타민제를 복용하다	**6** take vitamins	검사	**16** tests
전문의를 만나다	**7** see a specialist	물리치료	**17** physical therapy
침술을 받다	**8** get acupuncture	수술	**18** surgery
찜질 패드	**9** heating pad	상담	**19** counseling
가습기	**10** humidifier	치아교정기	**20** braces

A. I think ⎰ you should _____ [1–8].
⎱ you should use a/an _____ [9–14].
you need _____ [15–20].

B. I see.

A. What did the doctor say?

B. The doctor thinks ⎰ I should _____ [1–8].
⎱ I should use a/an _____ [9–14].
I need _____ [15–20].

Tell about medical advice a doctor gave you. What did the doctor say? Did you follow the advice?

약

아스피린	1	aspirin	목캔디	7	throat lozenges	알약	14	pill
정제감기약	2	cold tablets	제산정/제산제	8	antacid tablets	정제	15	tablet
비타민제	3	vitamins	분무식 충혈 완화제/	9	decongestant spray/	캡슐	16	capsule
진해 시럽/	4	cough syrup	비염용 스프레이		nasal spray	캐플릿	17	caplet
시럽제 기침약			안약	10	eye drops	찻숟가락	18	teaspoon
비아스피린 진통제	5	non-aspirin	연고	11	ointment	큰 스푼	19	tablespoon
		pain reliever	크림	12	cream/creme			
진해정/기침캔디	6	cough drops	로션	13	lotion			

[1–13]
A. What did the doctor say?
B. { She/He told me to take ____ [1–4] ____ /a ____ [5] ____ .
      She/He told me to use ____ [6–13] ____ .

[14–19]
A. What's the dosage?
B. One _____ every four hours.

What medicines in this lesson do you have at home? What other medicines do you have?

What do you take or use for a fever? a headache? a stomachache? a sore throat? a cold? a cough?

Tell about any medicines in your country that are different from the ones in this lesson.

의료 전문가

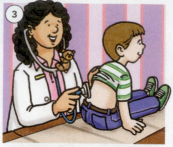

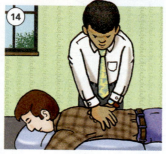
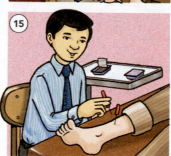

심장전문의	1 cardiologist	안과의사	7 ophthalmologist	정신과의사	12 psychiatrist
부인과의사	2 gynecologist	이비인후과전문의	8 ear, nose, and throat (ENT) specialist	위전문의	13 gastroenterologist
소아과의사	3 pediatrician			지압사	14 chiropractor
노인병 전문의	4 gerontologist	청력검사원	9 audiologist	침술사	15 acupuncturist
알레르기 전문의사	5 allergist	물리요법사	10 physical therapist	치열교정의사	16 orthodontist
정형외과의사	6 orthopedist	상담원/치료사	11 counselor/therapist		

A. I think you need to see a specialist.
   I'm going to refer you to a/an _____.
B. A/An _____?
A. Yes.

A. When is your next appointment with the _____?
B. It's at ....(time).... on ...(date)......

Do you or members of your family see any of these medical specialists? Which ones?

병원

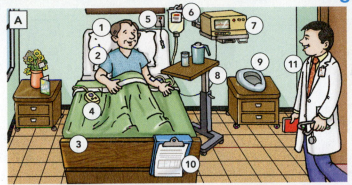

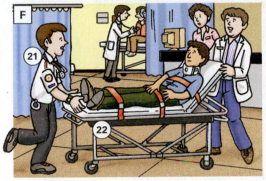
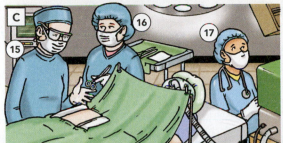

환자실	**A**	**patient's room**
환자	1	patient
환자복	2	hospital gown
병원 침대	3	hospital bed
침대 조절기	4	bed control
호출버튼	5	call button
정맥주사	6	I.V.
생명징후모니터	7	vital signs monitor
베드 테이블	8	bed table
환자용 변기	9	bed pan
진료차트	10	medical chart
의사/내과의사	11	doctor/physician

간호사실	**B**	**nurse's station**
간호사	12	nurse
영양사	13	dietitian
병원잡역부	14	orderly

수술실	**C**	**operating room**
외과의사	15	surgeon
외과 간호사	16	surgical nurse
마취전문의사	17	anesthesiologist

대기실	**D**	**waiting room**
자원봉사원	18	volunteer

분만실	**E**	**birthing room/ delivery room**
산과의사	19	obstetrician
조산사	20	midwife/nurse-midwife

응급실	**F**	**emergency room/ER**
응급구조대원	21	emergency medical technician/EMT
환자수송용침대	22	gurney

방사선과	**G**	**radiology department**
방사선과 기사	23	X-ray technician
방사선 의사	24	radiologist

실험실	**H**	**laboratory/lab**
임상병리사	25	lab technician

A. This is your _____ [2–10] .
B. I see.

A. Do you work here?
B. Yes. I'm a/an _____ [11–21, 23–25] .

A. Where's the _____ [11–21, 23–25] ?
B. She's/He's { in the _____ [A, C–H] .
                at the _____ [B] .

Tell about an experience you or a family member had in the hospital.

개인 위생

이를 닦다	**A**	**brush** *my* **teeth**		목욕하다	**E**	**bathe / take a bath**		머리를 빗다	**J**	**brush** *my* **hair**
칫솔	**1**	toothbrush		비누	**6**	soap		헤어브러쉬	**13**	(hair) brush
치약	**2**	toothpaste		목욕용 발포제	**7**	bubble bath		머리 모양을 내다	**K**	**style** *my* **hair**
치실질하다	**B**	**floss** *my* **teeth**		샤워를 하다	**F**	**take a shower**		헤어아이론	**14**	hot comb / curling iron
치실/플로스	**3**	dental floss		샤워 캡	**8**	shower cap		헤어스프레이	**15**	hairspray
양치질하다	**C**	**gargle**		머리를 감다	**G**	**wash** *my* **hair**		헤어겔	**16**	hair gel
양치질 물약/ 구강청정액	**4**	mouthwash		샴푸	**9**	shampoo		실핀	**17**	bobby pin
				모발 영양제/컨디셔너	**10**	conditioner / rinse		머리핀	**18**	barrette
치아를 하양게 하다	**D**	**whiten** *my* **teeth**		머리를 말리다	**H**	**dry** *my* **hair**		머리핀	**19**	hairclip
치아 화이트너	**5**	teeth whitener		헤어드라이기	**11**	hair dryer / blow dryer				
				머리를 빗다	**I**	**comb** *my* **hair**				
				빗	**12**	comb				

면도하다	L	shave
면도 크림	20	shaving cream
면도기	21	razor
면도날	22	razor blade
전기 면도기	23	electric shaver
지혈제 (연필 모양의)	24	styptic pencil
면도 후 로션	25	aftershave (lotion)

손톱 손질을 하다	M	do my nails
손톱 다듬는 줄	26	nail file
손톱 미는 줄	27	emery board
손톱깎이	28	nail clipper
손톱솔	29	nail brush
가위	30	scissors

매니큐어액	31	nail polish
매니큐어 제거제	32	nail polish remover

치장하다 …	N	put on . . .
방취제/ 디오도렌트/탈취제	33	deodorant
핸드 로션	34	hand lotion
바디로션	35	body lotion
파우더	36	powder
향수	37	cologne/ perfume
자외선 방지제	38	sunscreen

화장하다	O	put on makeup
볼연지	39	blush/rouge
파운데이션/ 기초화장품	40	foundation/ base
보습화장품	41	moisturizer
(화장) 분	42	face powder
아이라이너	43	eyeliner
아이섀도	44	eye shadow
마스카라	45	mascara
눈썹 연필	46	eyebrow pencil
립스틱	47	lipstick

구두를 닦다	P	polish my shoes
구두약	48	shoe polish
구두끈	49	shoelaces

[A–M, N (33–38), O, P]
A. What are you doing?
B. I'm _____ing.

[1, 8, 11–14, 17–19, 21–24, 26–30, 46, 49]
A. Excuse me. Where can I find _____(s)?
B. They're in the next aisle.

[2–7, 9, 10, 15, 16, 20, 25, 31–45, 47, 48]
A. Excuse me. Where can I find _____?
B. It's in the next aisle.

Which of these personal care products do you use?

You're going on a trip. Make a list of the personal care products you need to take with you.

아기 돌보기

먹이다	**A feed**
유아식	**1** baby food
턱받이	**2** bib
우유병/젖병	**3** bottle
고무 젖꼭지 (젖병의)	**4** nipple
분유	**5** formula
액체 비타민	**6** (liquid) vitamins
아기 기저귀를 바꾸다	**B change the baby's diaper**
일회용 기저귀	**7** disposable diaper
천 기저귀	**8** cloth diaper
기저귀용 옷핀	**9** diaper pin

아기 물휴지	**10** (baby) wipes
땀띠분	**11** baby powder
용변 연습용 팬티	**12** training pants
연고	**13** ointment
목욕시키다	**C bathe**
아기 샴푸	**14** baby shampoo
면봉	**15** cotton swab
아기 로션	**16** baby lotion
안다	**D hold**
노리개 젖꼭지	**17** pacifier
치아발육기	**18** teething ring
젖먹이다	**E nurse**

옷을 입히다	**F dress**
달래다	**G rock**
탁아소/ 놀이방	**19** child-care center
탁아소 직원	**20** child-care worker
흔들의자	**21** rocking chair
읽어주다	**H read to**
작은 찬장	**22** cubby
놀아주다	**I play with**
장난감	**23** toys

A. What are you doing?
B. { I'm ____[A, C–I]____ing the baby.
     I'm _____[B]_____ing.

A. Do we need anything from the store?
B. Yes. We need some more { [2–4, 7–9, 15, 17, 18] s
                            [1, 5, 6, 10–14, 16] .

In your opinion, which are better: cloth diapers or disposable diapers? Why?   Tell about baby products in your country.

학교 종류

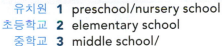

유치원	**1** preschool/nursery school	지역 사회 대학	**7** community college
초등학교	**2** elementary school	단과대학	**8** college
중학교	**3** middle school/ junior high school	대학교 (4년제)	**9** university
고등학교	**4** high school	대학원	**10** graduate school
성인학교	**5** adult school	법대	**11** law school
직업학교	**6** vocational school/trade school	의대	**12** medical school

A. Are you a student?
B. Yes. I'm in _____ [1–4, 8, 10–12] _____.

A. Are you a student?
B. Yes. I go to a/an _____ [5–7, 9] _____.

A. Is this apartment building near a/an _____?
B. Yes. _____ (name of school) _____ is nearby.

A. Tell me about your previous education.
B. I went to _____ (name of school) _____.
A. Did you like it there?
B. Yes. It was an excellent _____.

What types of schools are there in your community? What are their names, and where are they located?

What types of schools have you gone to?

Where? When? What did you study?

학교

교무실	**A**	(main) office
교장실	**B**	principal's office
양호실	**C**	nurse's office
진로 상담실	**D**	guidance office
교실	**E**	classroom
복도	**F**	hallway
사물함	**a**	locker
과학 실험실	**G**	science lab
체육관	**H**	gym/gymnasium
탈의실	**a**	locker room

트랙	**I**	track
관람석(지붕 없는)	**a**	bleachers
경기장/운동장	**J**	field
강당	**K**	auditorium
구내식당	**L**	cafeteria
도서관	**M**	library
교무직원	**1**	clerk/(school) secretary
교장	**2**	principal
양호 교사	**3**	(school) nurse
진로 상담 교사	**4**	(guidance) counselor

교사/선생님	**5**	teacher
교감	**6**	assistant principal/vice-principal
수위	**7**	security officer
과학 교사	**8**	science teacher
체육 교사	**9**	P.E. teacher
코치	**10**	coach
시설관리인	**11**	custodian
구내식당 종업원	**12**	cafeteria worker
구내식당 관리원	**13**	lunchroom monitor
학교사서	**14**	(school) librarian

A. Where are you going?
B. I'm going to the ___[A–D, G–M]___.
A. Do you have a hall pass?
B. Yes. Here it is.

A. Where's the ___[1–14]___?
B. He's/She's in the ___[A–M]___.

Describe the school where you study English.
Tell about the rooms, offices, and people.

Tell about differences between the school
in this lesson and schools in your country.

학과목

수학 **1** math/mathematics	컴퓨터 과학 **11** computer science
영어 **2** English	스페인어 **12** Spanish
역사 **3** history	불어 **13** French
지리 **4** geography	가정학 **14** home economics
정치 **5** government	공예 **15** industrial arts/shop
과학 **6** science	직업 교육 **16** business education
생물 **7** biology	체육 **17** physical education/P.E.
화학 **8** chemistry	운전자 교육 **18** driver's education/driver's ed
물리 **9** physics	미술 **19** art
보건위생 **10** health	음악 **20** music

A. What do you have next period?
B. **Math.** How about you?
A. **English.**
B. There's the bell. I've got to go.

What is/was your favorite subject? Why?

In your opinion, what's the most interesting subject? the most difficult subject? Why do you think so?

특별 과외 활동

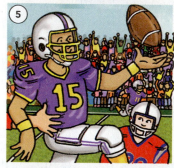

밴드	**1** band		학교신문/교지	**9** school newspaper
관현악단/오케스트라	**2** orchestra		졸업앨범	**10** yearbook
합창단	**3** choir/chorus		문예지	**11** literary magazine
드라마	**4** drama		시청각 직원	**12** A.V. crew
미식축구	**5** football		토론 클럽	**13** debate club
응원단	**6** cheerleading/pep squad		컴퓨터 클럽	**14** computer club
학생회	**7** student government		국제 클럽	**15** international club
지역 봉사	**8** community service		체스 클럽	**16** chess club

A. Are you going home right after school?
B. { No. I have ___[1–6]___ practice.
{ No. I have a ___[7–16]___ meeting.

What extracurricular activities do/did you participate in?

Which extracurricular activities in this lesson are there in schools in your country? What other activities are there?

수학

Arithmetic 산수

$$2+1=3 \qquad 8-3=5 \qquad 4\times2=8 \qquad 10\div2=5$$

덧셈 addition	뺄셈 subtraction	곱셈 multiplication	나눗셈 division
2 **plus** 1 **equals*** 3.	8 **minus** 3 **equals*** 5.	4 **times** 2 **equals*** 8.	10 **divided by** 2 **equals*** 5.

You can also say: **is**

A. How much is *two plus one?*
B. *Two plus one* equals / is *three.*

Make conversations for the arithmetic problems above and others.

Fractions 분수

1/4	1/3	1/2	2/3	3/4
one quarter / one fourth	one third	one half / half	two thirds	three quarters / three fourths

A. Is this on sale?
B. Yes. It's _____ off the regular price.

A. Is the gas tank almost empty?
B. It's about _____ full.

Percents 퍼센트

10% ten percent	50% fifty percent	75% seventy-five percent	100% one-hundred percent

A. How did you do on the test?
B. I got _____ percent of the answers right.

A. What's the weather forecast?
B. There's a _____ percent chance of rain.

Types of Math 수학의 종류

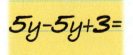  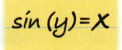 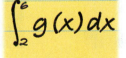 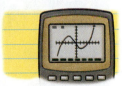

$$5y-5y+3=$$

algebra	geometry	trigonometry	calculus	statistics
대수	기하학	삼각법	미적분	통계

$$\sin(y)=x \qquad \int_2^6 g(x)\,dx$$

A. What math course are you taking this year?
B. I'm taking _____.

Are you good at math?

What math courses do / did you take in school?

Tell about something you bought on sale. How much off the regular price was it?

Research and discuss: What percentage of people in your country live in cities? live on farms? work in factories? vote in general elections?

계측 및 기하학 도형

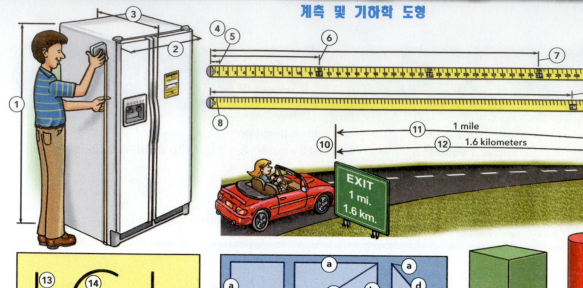

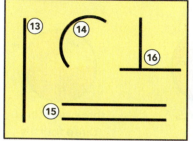

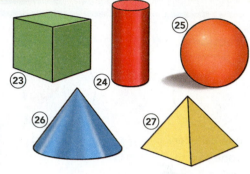

계측		Measurements
높이	1	height
폭/넓이	2	width
깊이	3	depth
길이	4	length
인치	5	inch
1 피트	6	foot–feet
야드(0.914 m)	7	yard
센티미터	8	centimeter
미터	9	meter
거리	10	distance
마일(1.609 km)	11	mile
킬로미터	12	kilometer

선		Lines
직선	13	straight line
곡선	14	curved line

평행선	15	parallel lines
수직선	16	perpendicular lines

기하학 도형		Geometric Shapes
정사각형/면	17	square
변		a side
직사각형	18	rectangle
길이		a length
폭/넓이		b width
대각선		c diagonal
직각 삼각형	19	right triangle
꼭지점		a apex
직각		b right angle
밑변		c base
빗변		d hypotenuse

이등변 삼각형	20	isosceles triangle
예각		a acute angle
둔각		b obtuse angle
원	21	circle
중심		a center
반지름		b radius
지름		c diameter
원주		d circumference
타원	22	ellipse/oval

입체도형		Solid Figures
정6면체	23	cube
원기둥	24	cylinder
구	25	sphere
원뿔	26	cone
각뿔	27	pyramid

[1–9]
A. What's the _____ [1–4] _____?
B. .... _____ [5–9] _____ (s).

[11–12]
A. What's the distance?
B. .... _____(s).

1 inch (1") = 2.54 centimeters (cm)
1 foot (1') = 0.305 meters (m)
1 yard (1 yd.) = 0.914 meters (m)
1 mile (mi.) = 1.6 kilometers (km)

[17–22]
A. Who can tell me what shape this is?
B. I can. It's a/an _____.

[23–27]
A. Who knows what figure this is?
B. I do. It's a/an _____.

[13–27]
A. This painting is magnificent!
B. Hmm. I don't think so. It just looks like a lot of _____s and _____s to me!

영어 및 작문

Types of Sentences & Parts of Speech 문장 형태와 품사

A Students study in the new library.
① ② ③ ④ ⑤

B Do they study hard?
⑥ ⑦

C Read page nine.

D This cake is fantastic!

진술형	**A** declarative	명사	**1** noun	형용사	**5** adjective
질문형	**B** interrogative	동사	**2** verb	대명사	**6** pronoun
명령형	**C** imperative	전치사	**3** preposition	부사	**7** adverb
감탄형	**D** exclamatory	관사	**4** article		

A. What type of sentence is this?
B. It's a/an ____[A–D]____ sentence.

A. What part of speech is this?
B. It's a/an ____[1–7]____.

Punctuation Marks & the Writing Process 구두점과 글쓰기 과정

마침표	**8** period	아이디어를 브레인스토밍하다	**16** brainstorm ideas
물음표	**9** question mark	아이디어(생각)를 정리하다	**17** organize *my* ideas
느낌표	**10** exclamation point	초고를 쓰다	**18** write a first draft
콤마	**11** comma	제목	**a** title
아포스트로피	**12** apostrophe	단락	**b** paragraph
인용 부호	**13** quotation marks	교정하다	**19** make corrections/revise/edit
콜론	**14** colon	피드백(평가)을 받다	**20** get feedback
세미콜론	**15** semi-colon	최종본을 쓰다	**21** write a final copy/rewrite

A. Did you find any mistakes?
B. Yes. You forgot to put a/an ____[8–15]____ in this sentence.

A. Are you working on your composition?
B. Yes. I'm ____[16–21]____ing.

문학 및 작문

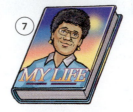

소설	**1**	fiction	에세이	**8**	essay	짧은 편지/메모	**15**	note
장편소설	**2**	novel	보고서	**9**	report	초청	**16**	invitation
단편소설	**3**	short story	잡지 기사	**10**	magazine article	감사편지	**17**	thank-you note
시(집)	**4**	poetry/poems	신문 기사	**11**	newspaper article	메모	**18**	memo
논픽션	**5**	non-fiction	사설	**12**	editorial	이메일	**19**	e-mail
전기	**6**	biography	편지	**13**	letter	즉석 메시지	**20**	instant message
자서전	**7**	autobiography	엽서	**14**	postcard			

A. What are you doing?
B. I'm writing { [1, 4, 5] .
a/an [2, 3, 6–20] .

What kind of literature do you like to read? What are some of your favorite books? Who is your favorite author?

Do you like to read newspapers and magazines? Which ones do you read?

Do you sometimes send or receive letters, postcards, notes, e-mail, or instant messages? Tell about the people you communicate with, and how.

지리

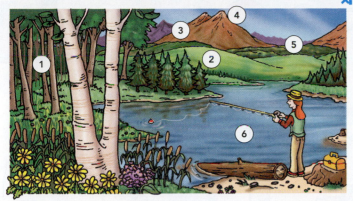

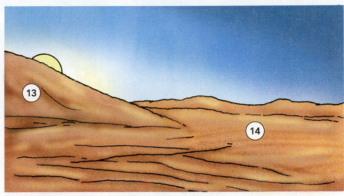

숲/삼림	**1**	forest/woods	시내	**9**	stream/brook	만	**17**	bay
언덕	**2**	hill	연못	**10**	pond	대양	**18**	ocean
산맥	**3**	mountain range	평원	**11**	plateau	섬	**19**	island
산봉오리	**4**	mountain peak	협곡	**12**	canyon	반도	**20**	peninsula
계곡	**5**	valley	모래언덕	**13**	dune/sand dune	열대 다우림	**21**	rainforest
호수	**6**	lake	사막	**14**	desert	강	**22**	river
평지/평원	**7**	plains	밀림/정글	**15**	jungle	폭포	**23**	waterfall
초원	**8**	meadow	해변	**16**	seashore/shore			

A. { Isn't this a beautiful _____?!
{ Aren't these beautiful _____s?!
B. Yes. It's/They're magnificent!

Tell about the geography of your country. Describe the different geographic features.

Have you seen some of the geographic features in this lesson? Which ones? Where?

과학

과학 기구	Science Equipment		자석	13	magnet
현미경	1	microscope	프리즘	14	prism
컴퓨터	2	computer	점적기	15	dropper
슬라이드	3	slide	화학약품	16	chemicals
(세균 배양용)페트리 접시	4	Petri dish	저울	17	balance
플라스크	5	flask	저울	18	scale
깔때기	6	funnel			
비커	7	beaker	과학적 방법	The Scientific Method	
시험관	8	test tube	문제를 제시하다	A	state the problem
족집게	9	forceps	가설을 세우다	B	form a hypothesis
집게	10	crucible tongs	(실험) 절차를 기획하다	C	plan a procedure
분젠 가스 버너	11	Bunsen burner	(실험) 절차를 실행하다	D	do a procedure
눈금 실린더	12	graduated cylinder	관찰을 기록하다	E	make/record observations
			결론을 내다	F	draw conclusions

A. What do we need to do this procedure?
B. We need a/an/the ___[1–18]___.

A. How is your experiment coming along?
B. I'm getting ready to ___[A–F]___.

Do you have experience with the scientific equipment in this lesson? Tell about it.

What science courses do/did you take in school?

Think of an idea for a science experiment.
What question about science do you want to answer? State the problem.
What do you think will happen in the experiment? Form a hypothesis.
How can you test your hypothesis? Plan a procedure.

우주

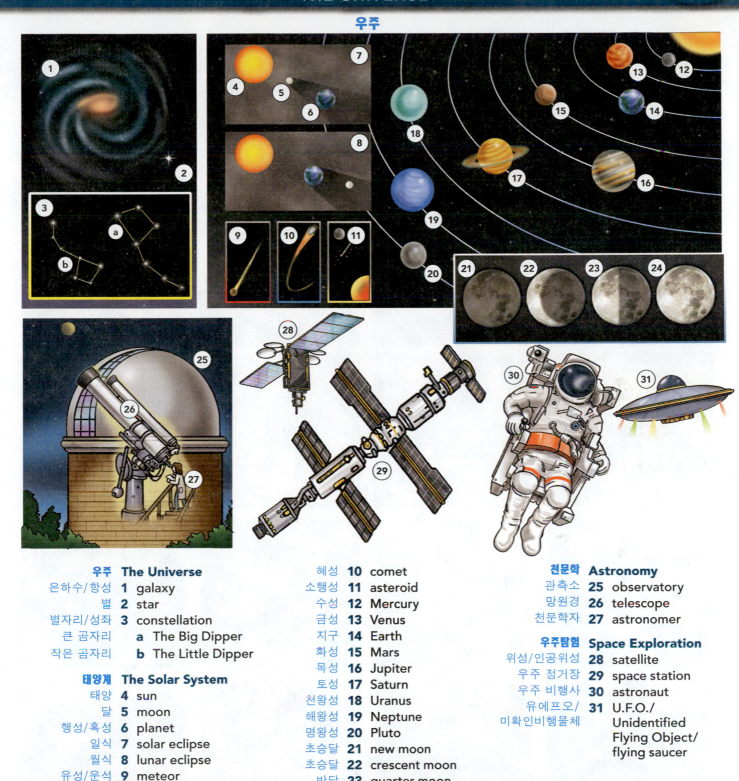

우주	**The Universe**
은하수/항성	**1** galaxy
별	**2** star
별자리/성좌	**3** constellation
큰 곰자리	**a** The Big Dipper
작은 곰자리	**b** The Little Dipper

태양계	**The Solar System**
태양	**4** sun
달	**5** moon
행성/혹성	**6** planet
일식	**7** solar eclipse
월식	**8** lunar eclipse
유성/운석	**9** meteor

혜성	**10** comet
소행성	**11** asteroid
수성	**12** Mercury
금성	**13** Venus
지구	**14** Earth
화성	**15** Mars
목성	**16** Jupiter
토성	**17** Saturn
천왕성	**18** Uranus
해왕성	**19** Neptune
명왕성	**20** Pluto
초승달	**21** new moon
초승달	**22** crescent moon
반달	**23** quarter moon
보름달	**24** full moon

천문학	**Astronomy**
관측소	**25** observatory
망원경	**26** telescope
천문학자	**27** astronomer

우주탐험	**Space Exploration**
위성/인공위성	**28** satellite
우주 정거장	**29** space station
우주 비행사	**30** astronaut
유에프오/ 미확인비행물체	**31** U.F.O./ Unidentified Flying Object/ flying saucer

[1–24]
A. Is that (a/an/the) _____?
B. I'm not sure. I think it might be (a/an/the) _____.

[28–30]
A. Is the _____ ready for tomorrow's launch?
B. Yes. "All systems are go!"

Pretend you are an astronaut traveling in space. What do you see?

Draw and name a constellation you are familiar with.

Do you think space exploration is important? Why?

Have you ever seen a U.F.O.? Do you believe there is life in outer space? Why?

직업 I

회계사	**1**	accountant	이발사	**9**	barber	어린이 놀이방 직원 **17** child day-care worker
남자배우/배우	**2**	actor	벽돌공	**10**	bricklayer/mason	컴퓨터 소프트웨어 **18** computer software engineer
여자배우	**3**	actress	사업가	**11**	businessman	엔지니어
건축가	**4**	architect	여성 사업가	**12**	businesswoman	건설공사 근로자 **19** construction worker
화가	**5**	artist	푸주한/정육점 주인	**13**	butcher	시설관리인 **20** custodian/janitor
조립공	**6**	assembler	목수	**14**	carpenter	고객서비스 **21** customer service representative
베이비시터/보모	**7**	babysitter	계산원	**15**	cashier	담당 직원
제과(제빵)기술자	**8**	baker	요리사/주방장	**16**	chef/cook	데이터 입력 직원 **22** data entry clerk

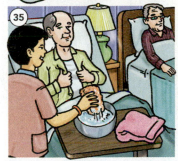

배달원	**23**	delivery person	음식 배급원	**30**	food-service worker	파출	**36**	home health aide/
항만 근로자	**24**	dockworker	현장주임/십장	**31**	foreman	간호조무사		home attendant
기사	**25**	engineer	정원사	**32**	gardener/landscaper	주부/가사를	**37**	homemaker
공장 근로자	**26**	factory worker	의상실 근로자	**33**	garment worker	꾸리는 사람		
농부	**27**	farmer	미용사	**34**	hairdresser	(호텔의)	**38**	housekeeper
소방관	**28**	firefighter	간호조무사	**35**	health-care aide/	객실관리인/		
어부	**29**	fisher			attendant	청소직원		

A. What do you do?
B. I'm an **accountant**. How about you?
A. I'm a **carpenter**.

Which of these occupations do you think are the most interesting? the most difficult? Why?

직업 II

보도 기자	**1** journalist/reporter
변호사	**2** lawyer
기계 기사	**3** machine operator
우편배달부	**4** mail carrier/letter carrier
지배인	**5** manager
미조술사	**6** manicurist
수리공/자동차 수리공	**7** mechanic

의사 보조원	**8** medical assistant/ physician assistant
배달부	**9** messenger/courier
운송업자	**10** mover
음악가	**11** musician
페인트공	**12** painter
약사	**13** pharmacist

사진사	**14** photographer
조종사	**15** pilot
경찰	**16** police officer
우체국 직원	**17** postal worker
응접원	**18** receptionist
수리공	**19** repairperson
판매원/점원	**20** salesperson

환경미화원 **21** sanitation worker/ trash collector	상점 주인 **27** store owner/ shopkeeper	여행사 직원 **33** travel agent
비서 **22** secretary	지도주임(학교의) **28** supervisor	트럭 운전사 **34** truck driver
경비원/보안 검색원 **23** security guard	재단사 **29** tailor	수의사 **35** veterinarian/vet
군인 **24** serviceman	선생님/교사 **30** teacher/instructor	웨이터 **36** waiter/server
여군 **25** servicewoman	전화 판매 홍보원 **31** telemarketer	웨이트리스 **37** waitress/server
창고 담당 직원 **26** stock clerk	번역사/통역사 **32** translator/interpreter	용접공 **38** welder

A. What's your occupation?
B. I'm a **journalist**.
A. A **journalist**?
B. Yes. That's right.

A. Are you still a _____?
B. No. I'm a _____.
A. Oh. That's interesting.

A. What kind of job would you like in the future?
B. I'd like to be a _____.

Do you work? What's your occupation?

What are the occupations of people in your family?

직업 기술과 활동들

연기하다 **1** act
조립하다 **2** assemble *components*
환자를 돕다 **3** assist *patients*
굽다 **4** bake
짓다/만들다 **5** build *things*/construct *things*
청소하다 **6** clean
요리하다 **7** cook
피자를 배달하다 **8** deliver *pizzas*
건물을 설계하다 **9** design *buildings*
그리다 **10** draw

트럭을 운전하다 **11** drive *a truck*
서류를 철하다/정리하다 **12** file
비행기를 조종하다 **13** fly *an airplane*
식물을 기르다 **14** grow *vegetables*
건물을 경비하다 **15** guard *buildings*
레스토랑을 운영하다 **16** manage *a restaurant*
잔디를 깎다 **17** mow *lawns*
설비 기계를 작동하다 **18** operate *equipment*
페인트칠하다 **19** paint
피아노를 연주하다 **20** play the *piano*

음식을 준비하다	**21** prepare *food*		노인을 보살피다	**29** take care of *elderly people*
물건을 수리하다	**22** repair *things*/fix *things*		재고 목록을 작성하다	**30** take inventory
차를 팔다	**23** sell *cars*		가르치다	**31** teach
음식을 가져다 주다	**24** serve *food*		통역하다	**32** translate
바느질하다	**25** sew		타이프를 치다	**33** type
노래하다	**26** sing		금전등록기를 사용하다	**34** use *a cash register*
스페인어로 말하다	**27** speak *Spanish*		접시를 닦다	**35** wash *dishes*
사람을 지도하다	**28** supervise *people*		글을 쓰다	**36** write

A. Can you **act**?
B. Yes, I can.

A. Do you know how to _____?
B. Yes. I've been _____ing for years.

A. Tell me about your skills.
B. I can _____, and I can _____.

Tell about your job skills.
What can you do?

일자리 찾기

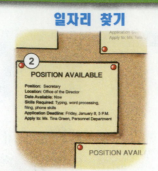

직업 광고 형태들	Types of Job Ads
구인 광고판	1 help wanted sign
일자리 공고	2 job notice/ job announcement
분야별 안내광고	3 classified ad/want ad

직업 광고 줄임말	Job Ad Abbreviations
전임의	4 full-time
비상근의	5 part-time
지원 가능한	6 available
시간	7 hour
월요일부터 금요일	8 Monday through Friday
저녁	9 evenings
이전의	10 previous
경험	11 experience
필수	12 required
우수한	13 excellent

일자리 찾기	Job Search
광고에 응답하다	A respond to an ad
정보를 구하다	B request information
면접을 요청하다	C request an interview
이력서를 준비하다	D prepare a resume
적절하게 옷을 입다	E dress appropriately
지원서를 작성하다	F fill out an application (form)
면접하러 가다	G go to an interview
당신의 기술과 적성을 이야기하다	H talk about your skills and qualifications
당신의 경험을 이야기하다	I talk about your experience
월급을 묻다	J ask about the salary
혜택을 묻다	K ask about the benefits
감사편지를 쓰다	L write a thank-you note
고용되다	M get hired

A. How did you find your job?
B. I found it through a _____[1–3]_____.

A. How was your job interview?
B. It went very well.
A. Did you _____[D–F, H–M]_____?
B. Yes, I did.

Tell about a job you are familiar with. What are the skills and qualifications required for the job? What are the hours? What is the salary?

Tell about how people you know found their jobs.

Tell about your own experience with a job search or a job interview.

일터

응접실	**A** reception area	우편 저울	**6** postal scale	사무보조원	**22** administrative assistant
회의실	**B** conference room	우편요금 별납 인쇄기	**7** postage meter	사무실 관리인	**23** office manager
우편물실	**C** mailroom	사환	**8** office assistant	비품함	**24** supply cabinet
작업실	**D** work area	우편함	**9** mailbox	물품함	**25** storage cabinet
사무실	**E** office	개인사무공간	**10** cubicle	자판기/자동판매기	**26** vending machine
비품실	**F** supply room	회전의자	**11** swivel chair	냉수기	**27** water cooler
물품 보관실	**G** storage room	타자기	**12** typewriter	커피 자판기	**28** coffee machine
직원 휴게실	**H** employee lounge	계산기	**13** adding machine	게시판	**29** message board
코트걸이/벽걸이	**1** coat rack	복사기	**14** copier/photocopier	메시지를 받다	**a** take a message
옷장	**2** coat closet	문서 분쇄기	**15** paper shredder	발표하다	**b** give a presentation
응접담당자	**3** receptionist	종이 절단기	**16** paper cutter	우편물을 분류하다	**c** sort the mail
회의용 테이블	**4** conference table	문서정리원	**17** file clerk	복사하다	**d** make copies
발표 게시판	**5** presentation board	서류철 캐비닛	**18** file cabinet	서류철	**e** file
		비서	**19** secretary	타이핑을 하다	**f** type a letter
		컴퓨터 작업대	**20** computer workstation		
		고용주	**21** employer/boss		

[A–H]
A. Where's ____(name)____?
B. He's/She's in the ____.

[1–29]
A. What do you think of the new ____?
B. He's/She's/It's very nice.

[a–f]
A. What's ____(name)____ doing?
B. He's/She's ____ing.

Describe a workplace you are familiar with. Tell about the rooms, the areas, and the employees.

사무실 용품 및 집기

책상	**1** desk	일정관리 수첩	**12** organizer/ personal planner	타자기 카트리지	**25** typewriter cartridge
스테이플러	**2** stapler	고무 밴드	**13** rubber band	잉크 카트리지	**26** ink cartridge
결재서류함	**3** letter tray/ stacking tray	종이 클립	**14** paper clip	고무 스탬프	**27** rubber stamp
회전식 명함 파일	**4** rotary card file	스테이플러 알	**15** staple	인주/스탬프	**28** ink pad
책상 깔개	**5** desk pad	압정	**16** thumbtack	고체풀	**29** glue stick
업무일정 수첩	**6** appointment book	압핀	**17** pushpin	접착제/풀	**30** glue
필기판(집게 달린)	**7** clipboard	법률 용지철	**18** legal pad	고무풀	**31** rubber cement
메모장	**8** note pad/ memo pad	서류철/화일홀더	**19** file folder	수정액	**32** correction fluid
자동 연필깎기	**9** electric pencil sharpener	색인카드	**20** index card	스카치 테이프	**33** cellophane tape/ clear tape
책상 달력	**10** desk calendar	편지봉투	**21** envelope	포장 테이프	**34** packing tape/ sealing tape
포스트잇철	**11** Post-It note pad	편지지	**22** stationery/ letterhead (paper)		
		우송 대봉투	**23** mailer		
		수신인 주소 라벨	**24** mailing label		

A. My desk is a mess! I can't find my __[2-12]__ !
B. Here it is next to your __[2-12]__ .

A. Could you get some more __[13-21, 23-29]__ s/ __[22, 30-34]__ from the supply room?
B. Some more __[13-21, 23-29]__ s/ __[22, 30-34]__ ? Sure. I'd be happy to.

Which supplies and equipment do you use? What do you use them for?

Which supplies in this lesson do you have at home? at school?

공장

출퇴근시간 기록기	**1**	time clock
근무시간기록표	**2**	time cards
라커룸	**3**	locker room
조립라인	**4**	(assembly) line
공장 근로자	**5**	(factory) worker
작업대	**6**	work station
생산 라인 관리인	**7**	line supervisor
품질관리감독관	**8**	quality control supervisor

기계	**9**	machine
컨베이어 벨트	**10**	conveyor belt
창고	**11**	warehouse
포장 담당 직원	**12**	packer
지게차	**13**	forklift
화물용 승강기	**14**	freight elevator
노조 게시판	**15**	union notice
건의함	**16**	suggestion box

출고부서	**17**	shipping department
출고 담당 직원	**18**	shipping clerk
손수레	**19**	hand truck/ dolly
적재장	**20**	loading dock
경리부	**21**	payroll office
인사부	**22**	personnel office

A. Excuse me. I'm a new employee. Where's/Where are the _____?
B. Next to/Near/In/On the _____.

A. Have you seen *Tony*?
B. Yes. *He's* in/on/at/next to/near the _____.

Are there any factories where you live? What kind? What are the working conditions there?

What products do factories in your country produce?

건설 현장

큰 망치	1	sledgehammer
곡괭이	2	pickax
삽	3	shovel
일륜수레	4	wheelbarrow
착암용 드릴	5	jackhammer/ pneumatic drill
설계도	6	blueprints
사다리	7	ladder
줄자	8	tape measure
공구벨트	9	toolbelt
흙손	10	trowel
콘크리트 믹서	11	cement mixer
시멘트	a	cement

비계목/ 작업발판대	12	scaffolding
덤프 트럭	13	dump truck
선두 적하기	14	front-end loader
기중기/크레인	15	crane
체리픽커/ 이동식 크레인	16	cherry picker
불도저	17	bulldozer
굴착기/백호/ 포클레인	18	backhoe
콘크리트 믹서 트럭	19	concrete mixer truck
콘크리트	a	concrete

픽업 트럭	20	pickup truck
트레일러	21	trailer
건식 벽체	22	drywall
목재	23	wood/lumber
합판	24	plywood
단열재/절연체	25	insulation
전선	26	wire
벽돌	27	brick
지붕널	28	shingle
파이프	29	pipe
도리	30	girder/beam

A. Could you get me that/those ___[1–10]___ ?
B. Sure.

A. Watch out for that ___[11–21]___ !
B. Oh! Thanks for the warning!

A. Do we have enough ___[22–26]___ / ___[27–30]___ s?
B. I think so.

What building materials is your home made of?
When was it built?

Describe a construction site near your home or school.
Tell about the construction equipment and the materials.

직업 안전

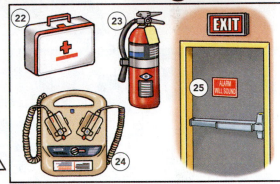

안전모	1	hard hat/helmet
귀마개	2	earplugs
물안경	3	goggles
안전 조끼	4	safety vest
안전화	5	safety boots
발가락 보호대	6	toe guard
등 받침대	7	back support
안전 귀마개	8	safety earmuffs
머리망	9	hairnet

마스크	10	mask
고무 장갑	11	latex gloves
방독마스크	12	respirator
보안경	13	safety glasses
가연성의	14	flammable
유독한	15	poisonous
부식성의	16	corrosive
방사성의	17	radioactive
위험한	18	dangerous

사고 위험성이 있는	19	hazardous
생물학적 위험	20	biohazard
전기 위험	21	electrical hazard
구급 상자	22	first-aid kit
소화기	23	fire extinguisher
세동 제거기	24	defibrillator
비상출구	25	emergency exit

A. Don't forget to wear your ___[1–13]___!
B. Thanks for reminding me.

A. Be careful!
- That material is ___[14–17]___!
- That machine is ___[18]___!
- That work area is ___[19]___!
- That's a ___[20]___! / That's an ___[21]___!

B. Thanks for the warning.

A. Where's the ___[22–25]___?
B. It's over there.

Have you ever used any of the safety equipment in this lesson? What have you used? When? Where?

Where do you see people using safety equipment in your community?

대중 교통

버스		A bus		기차		B train		지하철		C subway
버스 정류장	1	bus stop		기차역	11	train station		지하철 역	19	subway station
버스 노선	2	bus route		매표소	12	ticket window		지하철 토큰	20	(subway) token
승객	3	passenger/rider		착발 안내판	13	arrival and departure board		회전식 개찰구	21	turnstile
(버스)요금	4	(bus) fare						승차표	22	fare card
환승권	5	transfer		안내 데스크	14	information booth		발권기/발매기	23	fare card machine
버스 운전사	6	bus driver		일정표/시간표	15	schedule/ timetable		택시		D taxi
버스 정거장	7	bus station						택시 승차장	24	taxi stand
발권창구	8	ticket counter		플랫폼	16	platform		택시	25	taxi/cab/taxicab
승차권	9	ticket		트랙/선로	17	track		미터기	26	meter
수하물칸	10	baggage compartment/ luggage compartment		차장	18	conductor		택시 운전사	27	cab driver/taxi driver
								페리		E ferry

[A–E]
A. How are you going to get there?
B. { I'm going to take the __[A–C, E]__ .
     I'm going to take a __[D]__ .

[1, 7, 8, 10–19, 21, 23–25]
A. Excuse me. Where's the _____?
B. Over there.

How do you get to different places in your community?
Describe public transportation where you live.

In your country, can you travel far by train or by bus? Where can you go? How much do tickets cost? Describe the buses and trains.

차량 종류

세단	**1**	sedan
해치백	**2**	hatchback
컨버터블/	**3**	convertible
지붕을 접을 수 있는 차		
스포츠 카	**4**	sports car
하이브리드	**5**	hybrid
스테이션왜건	**6**	station wagon
스포츠 범용 차	**7**	S.U.V. (sport utility vehicle)

지프	**8**	jeep
밴	**9**	van
미니밴	**10**	minivan
픽업 트럭	**11**	pickup truck
리무진	**12**	limousine
견인차	**13**	tow truck
레크리에이션용 차량	**14**	R.V. (recreational vehicle)/camper
이삿짐 트럭	**15**	moving van

트럭	**16**	truck
트레일러 트럭	**17**	tractor trailer/ semi
두발 자전거	**18**	bicycle/bike
스쿠터	**19**	motor scooter
모터 자전거	**20**	moped
오토바이	**21**	motorcycle

A. What kind of vehicle are you looking for?
B. I'm looking for a **sedan**.

A. Do you drive a/an _____?
B. No. I drive a/an _____.

A. I just saw an accident between a/an _____ and a/an _____!
B. Was anybody hurt?
A. No. Fortunately, nobody was hurt.

What are the most common types of vehicles in your country?

What's your favorite type of vehicle? Why? In your opinion, which company makes the best one?

차 부품과 관리

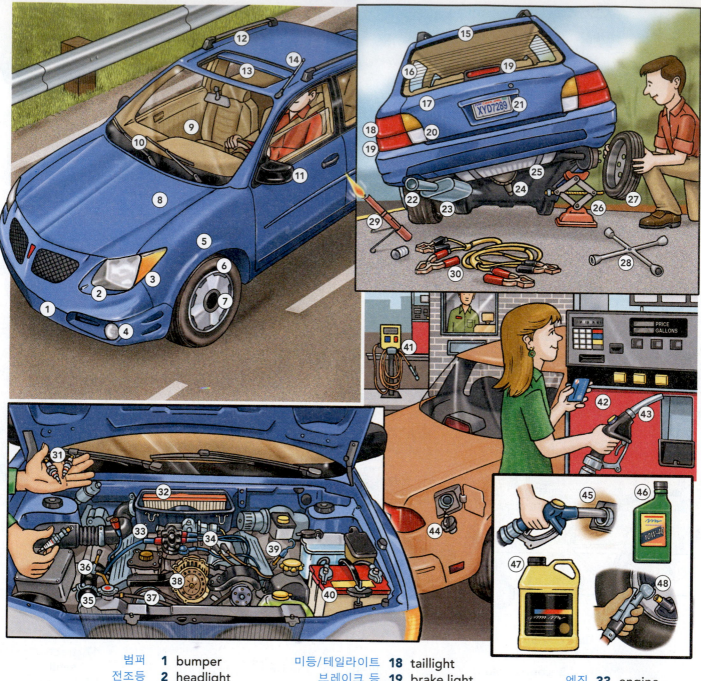

범퍼	1	bumper
전조등	2	headlight
방향지시등	3	turn signal
주차등	4	parking light
펜더	5	fender
타이어	6	tire
휠캡	7	hubcap
(자동차의) 엔진 뚜껑/보닛	8	hood
앞 유리창	9	windshield
앞 유리창 와이퍼	10	windshield wipers
사이드 미러	11	side mirror
지붕짐받이	12	roof rack
선루프	13	sunroof
안테나	14	antenna
뒷창(자동차의)	15	rear window
뒷창 서리제거장치	16	rear defroster
트렁크	17	trunk

미등/테일라이트	18	taillight
브레이크 등	19	brake light
후진등	20	backup light
번호판	21	license plate
배기관	22	tailpipe/ exhaust pipe
소음기	23	muffler
트랜스미션	24	transmission
연료탱크	25	gas tank
잭	26	jack
예비 타이어/ 스페어 타이어	27	spare tire
럭 렌치	28	lug wrench
비상 조명 장치	29	flare
점퍼 케이블 (자동차 배터리 충전용)	30	jumper cables
점화플러그	31	spark plugs
공기 여과기	32	air filter

엔진	33	engine
연료 분사 시스템	34	fuel injection system
냉각기 (자동차의)	35	radiator
라디에이터 호스	36	radiator hose
팬 밸트	37	fan belt
발전기	38	alternator
오일 계량봉	39	dipstick
배터리	40	battery
공기펌프	41	air pump
주유펌프	42	gas pump
분출구	43	nozzle
연료통 뚜껑	44	gas cap
휘발유	45	gas
오일(에진의)	46	oil
냉각제	47	coolant
공기	48	air

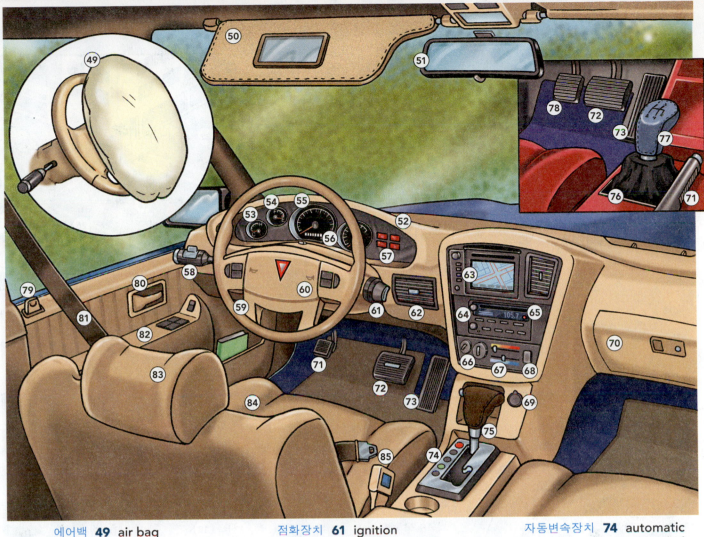

에어백	49	air bag
햇빛 가리개	50	visor
백미러	51	rearview mirror
계기반	52	dashboard/ instrument panel
온도계	53	temperature gauge
연료계기판	54	gas gauge/ fuel gauge
속도계기판	55	speedometer
주행거리계기판	56	odometer
비상등	57	warning lights
방향지시기	58	turn signal
운전대	59	steering wheel
경적/클랙슨	60	horn

점화장치	61	ignition
통풍구	62	vent
항법 장치	63	navigation system
라디오	64	radio
시디 플레이어	65	CD player
히터	66	heater
에어컨	67	air conditioning
서리제거기	68	defroster
전원 콘센트	69	power outlet
사물함	70	glove compartment
비상 브레이크	71	emergency brake
브레이크 페달	72	brake (pedal)
엑셀러레이터/ 가속 페달	73	accelerator/ gas pedal

자동변속장치	74	automatic transmission
변속기어	75	gearshift
수동변속장치	76	manual transmission
수동변속레버	77	stickshift
클러치	78	clutch
차문 잠금쇠/도어 록	79	door lock
차문 손잡이	80	door handle
안전벨트/ 어깨벨트	81	shoulder harness
팔걸이	82	armrest
머리받침대	83	headrest
좌석	84	seat
좌석벨트	85	seat belt

[2, 3, 9–16, 24, 35–39, 49–85]
A. What's the matter with your car?
B. The _____(s) is/are broken.

[45–48]
A. Can I help you?
B. {Yes. My car needs ___[45–47]___.
{Yes. My tires need ___[48]___.

[1, 2, 4–15, 17–23, 25]
A. I was just in a car accident!
B. Oh, no! Were you hurt?
A. No. But my _____(s) was/were damaged.

In your opinion, what are the most important features to look for when you buy a car?

Do you own a car? What kind? Tell about any repairs your car has needed.

고속도로 및 도로

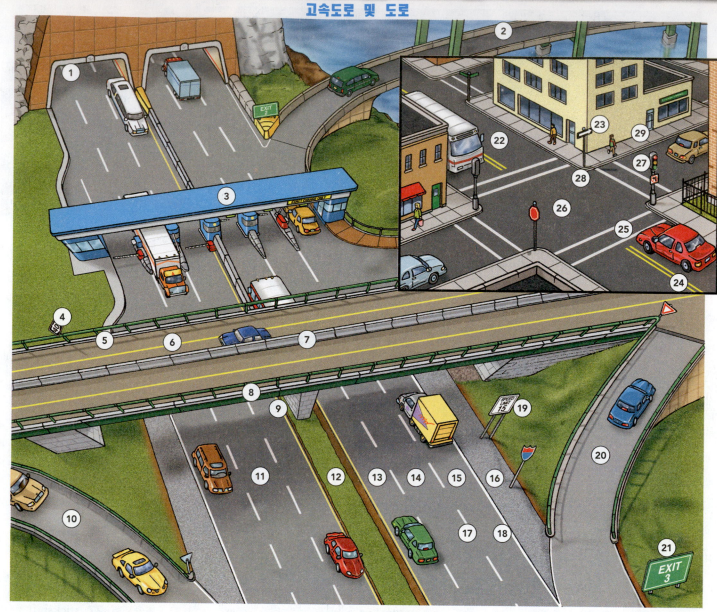

터널	**1** tunnel	중앙분리대	**12** median	일방통행로	**23** one-way street
다리	**2** bridge	좌측 차선	**13** left lane	이중 황색선	**24** double yellow line
요금징수소	**3** tollbooth	중앙 차선/2차선	**14** middle lane/ center lane	횡단보도	**25** crosswalk
도로표지판	**4** route sign	우측 차선	**15** right lane	교차로	**26** intersection
고속도로	**5** highway	갓길/노견	**16** shoulder	교통신호등	**27** traffic light/ traffic signal
도로	**6** road	점선	**17** broken line	모퉁이	**28** corner
분리대	**7** divider/barrier	실선	**18** solid line	블록	**29** block
고가도로	**8** overpass	속도제한 표지	**19** speed limit sign		
지하도로	**9** underpass	출구 램프	**20** exit (ramp)		
진입로	**10** entrance ramp/ on ramp	출구표지	**21** exit sign		
주간고속도로	**11** interstate (highway)	도로/거리	**22** street		

[1–28]
A. Where's the accident?
B. It's on / in / at / near the _____.

Describe a highway you travel on.

Describe an intersection near where you live.

In your area, on which highways and streets do most accidents occur? Why are these places dangerous?

움직임 전치사

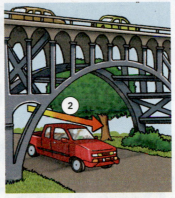

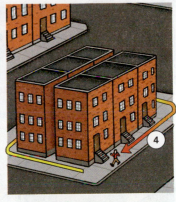

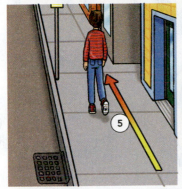

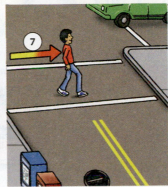

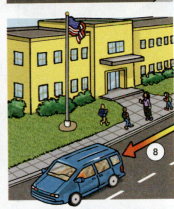

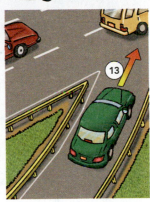

~위로	**1** over	위를 향해	**5** up	~로 타	**9** on
~의 밑으로	**2** under	아래를 향해	**6** down	~를 내려	**10** off
~를 통해	**3** through	~를 건너	**7** across	~의 안으로	**11** into
~를 돌아	**4** around	~를 지나	**8** past	~의 밖으로	**12** out of
				~로 들어서	**13** onto

[1–8]
A. Go **over** the bridge.
B. **Over** the bridge?
A. Yes.

[9–13]
A. I can't talk right now. I'm getting **on** a train.
B. You're getting **on** a train?
A. Yes. I'll call you later.

What places do you go past on your way to school?   Tell how to get to different places from your home or your school.

교통 표지판과 방향

교통 표지판	Traffic Signs		학교앞 건널목	11	school crossing	도로주행테스트	Road Test
정지	1 stop		합류로	12	merging traffic	지시사항	Instructions
좌회전 금지	2 no left turn		양보	13	yield	좌회전하세요.	21 Turn left.
우회전 금지	3 no right turn		우회로	14	detour	우회전하세요.	22 Turn right.
U턴 금지	4 no U-turn		우천시 미끄러움	15	slippery when wet	똑바로 가세요.	23 Go straight.
우회전 전용	5 right turn only		장애인 주차 전용	16	handicapped	평행 주차를 하세요.	24 Parallel park.
진입금지	6 do not enter				parking only	3점식 회전을	25 Make a
일방통행	7 one way					하세요.	3-point turn.
막다른 골목	8 dead end/no outlet		나침반 방향		Compass Directions	수신호를	26 Use hand
보행자 횡단	9 pedestrian crossing		북	17	north	사용하세요.	signals.
철도 건널목	10 railroad crossing		남	18	south		
			서	19	west		
			동	20	east		

[1–16]
A. Careful! That sign says "**stop**"!
B. Oh. Thanks.

[17–20]
A. Which way should I go?
B. Go **north**.

[21–26]
A. Turn **right**.
B. Turn **right**?
A. Yes.

Which of these traffic signs are in your neighborhood?
What other traffic signs do you usually see?

Describe any differences between traffic signs in
different countries you know.

공항

체크인	A	Check-In
탑승권	1	ticket
티켓 카운터	2	ticket counter
발매인	3	ticket agent
여행가방	4	suitcase
이착륙 모니터	5	arrival and departure monitor

보안 검색	B	Security
보안 검색대	6	security checkpoint
금속탐지기	7	metal detector
보안 검색관	8	security officer
X-레이 기계	9	X-ray machine
기내 휴대 수화물	10	carry-on bag

탑승구	C	The Gate
체크인 카운터	11	check-in counter
탑승권	12	boarding pass
탑승구	13	gate
탑승권	14	boarding area

수하물 찾기	D	Baggage Claim
수하물 찾는 곳	15	baggage claim (area)
수하물 회전 컨베이어	16	baggage carousel
수하물	17	baggage
짐 수레	18	baggage cart/ luggage cart
간이 짐수레	19	luggage carrier
옷가방	20	garment bag
수하물표	21	baggage claim check

세관 및 입국심사	E	Customs and Immigration
세관	22	customs
세관원	23	customs officer
세관 신고서	24	customs declaration form
출입국관리소	25	immigration
출입국관리소 직원	26	immigration officer
여권	27	passport
비자	28	visa

[2, 3, 5–9, 11, 13–16, 22, 23, 25, 26]
A. Excuse me. Where's the _____?*
B. Right over there.

* With 22 and 25 use: Excuse me. Where's _____?

[1, 4, 10, 12, 17–21, 24, 27, 28]
A. Oh, no! I think I've lost my _____!
B. I'll help you look for it.

Describe an airport you are familiar with. Tell about the check-in area, the security area, the gates, and the baggage claim area.

Have you ever gone through Customs and Immigration? Tell about your experience.

항공기 여행

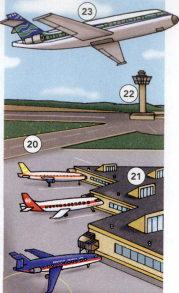

조종실	1 cockpit
조종사	2 pilot/captain
부조종사	3 co-pilot
화장실	4 lavatory/bathroom
승무원	5 flight attendant
기내 선반 짐칸	6 overhead compartment
통로	7 aisle
창가쪽 좌석	8 window seat
중간좌석	9 middle seat
통로쪽 좌석	10 aisle seat
좌석벨트 착용신호	11 Fasten Seat Belt sign
금연신호	12 No Smoking sign
호출 버튼	13 call button
산소 마스크	14 oxygen mask
비상구	15 emergency exit
트레이(테이블)	16 tray (table)
비상시 행동지침서	17 emergency instruction card
위생봉투	18 air sickness bag

구명조끼	19 life vest/life jacket
활주로	20 runway
터미널	21 terminal (building)
중앙관제탑	22 control tower
항공기/제트여객기	23 airplane/plane/jet

신발을 벗다	A take off your shoes
주머니를 비우다	B empty your pockets
컨베이어 벨트에 짐을 올려놓다	C put your bag on the conveyor belt
트레이에 컴퓨터를 놓다	D put your computer in a tray
금속탐지기를 걸어서 통과하다	E walk through the metal detector
탑승구에서 탑승 소속을 하다	F check in at the gate
탑승권을 받다	G get your boarding pass
비행기에 탑승하다	H board the plane
휴대 수화물을 짐칸에 넣다	I stow your carry-on bag
좌석을 찾다	J find your seat
좌석 벨트를 착용하다	K fasten your seat belt

[1–23]
A. Where's the _____?
B. In/On/Next to/Behind/In front of/ Above/Below the _____.

[A–K]
A. Please _____.
B. All right. Certainly.

Have you ever flown in an airplane? Tell about a flight you took.

Be an airport security officer! Give passengers instructions as they go through the security area. Now, be a flight attendant! Give passengers instructions before take-off.

호텔

도어맨	**1** doorman	투숙객	**10** guest	제빙기	**19** ice machine
대리 주차	**2** valet parking	접수계 데스크	**11** concierge desk	복도	**20** hall/hallway
주차 관리원	**3** parking attendant	접수계	**12** concierge	방 열쇠	**21** room key
벨보이	**4** bellhop	식당	**13** restaurant	객실관리수레	**22** housekeeping cart
짐 수레	**5** luggage cart	회의실	**14** meeting room		
급사장	**6** bell captain	선물가게	**15** gift shop	객실관리인	**23** housekeeper
로비	**7** lobby	수영장	**16** pool	객실	**24** guest room
프런트	**8** front desk	체력단련실	**17** exercise room	룸서비스	**25** room service
접수 담당자	**9** desk clerk	엘리베이터	**18** elevator		

A. Where do you work?
B. I work at the *Grand* Hotel.
A. What do you do there?
B. I'm a/an ____[1, 3, 4, 6, 9, 12, 23]____ .

A. Excuse me. Where's the ____[1–19, 22, 23]____ ?
B. Right over there.
A. Thanks.

Tell about a hotel you are familiar with. Describe the place and the people.

In your opinion, which hotel employee has the most interesting job? the most difficult job? Why?

취미, 수공예 및 게임

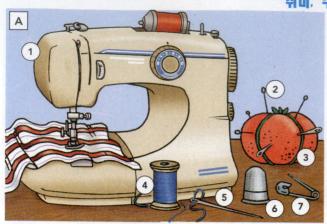

재봉하다	**A**	**sew**	물감	**D**	**paint**	바늘 레이스를 하다	**G**	**do needlepoint**

재봉하다 **A sew**
재봉틀 **1** sewing machine
핀/못바늘 **2** pin
바늘꽂이방석/ **3** pin cushion
바늘겨레
(한꾸리의) 실 **4** (spool of) thread
(바느질) 바늘 **5** (sewing) needle
골무 **6** thimble
옷핀 **7** safety pin

뜨개질하다 **B knit**
뜨개질 바늘 **8** knitting needle
털실 **9** yarn

크로셰 뜨개실 **C crochet**
크로셰 코바늘 **10** crochet hook

물감 **D paint**
그림붓 **11** paintbrush
이젤 **12** easel
캔버스 **13** canvas
물감 **14** paint
유화 물감 **a** oil paint
수채화 물감 **b** watercolor

그리다 **E draw**
스케치북 **15** sketch book
색연필(세트) **16** (set of) colored pencils
그림 연필 **17** drawing pencil

자수를 하다 **F do embroidery**
자수 **18** embroidery

바늘 레이스를 하다 **G do needlepoint**
바늘로 뜬 자수 **19** needlepoint
틀 **20** pattern

목공예를 하다 **H do woodworking**
목공예도구세트 **21** woodworking kit

종이접기를 하다 **I do origami**
종이접기용 종이 **22** origami paper

도자기를 만들다 **J make pottery**
점토 **23** clay
녹로(도공용) **24** potter's wheel

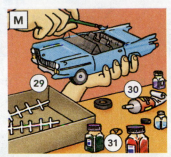

우표를 수집하다 **K collect stamps**
우표 앨범 **25** stamp album
돋보기 **26** magnifying glass

동전을 수집하다 **L collect coins**
동전카탈로그 **27** coin catalog
동전수집 **28** coin collection

모형을 짜맞추다 **M build models**
모형 세트 **29** model kit
접착제 **30** glue
아크릴 그림 물감 **31** acrylic paint

야조 관찰을 가다 **N go bird-watching**
쌍안경 **32** binoculars
휴대용 도감 **33** field guide

카드 놀이를 하다 **O play cards**
카드 (한벌) **34** (deck of) cards
클럽(카드놀이의) **a** club
다이아몬드 **b** diamond
하트 **c** heart
스페이드 **d** spade

보드 게임을 하다 **P play board games**
서양장기 **35** chess
체커 **36** checkers
백개먼 **37** backgammon
(서양 주사위놀이)

모노폴리 **38** Monopoly
(부동산 취득 게임)
주사위 **a** dice
스크래블 **39** Scrabble

온라인으로 들어가다/ **Q go online/ browse the Web/ "surf" the net**
웹을 검색하다
웹 브라우저 **40** web browser
웹 주소 **41** web address/URL

사진 촬영 **R photography**
카메라 **42** camera

천문학 **S astronomy**
망원경 **43** telescope

A. What do you like to do in your free time?
B. I like to ___[A–Q]___ .
   I enjoy ___[R, S]___ .

A. May I help you?
B. Yes, please. I'd like to buy (a/an) ___[1–34, 42, 43]___ .

A. What do you want to do?
B. Let's play ___[35–39]___ .
A. Good idea!

Do you like to do any of these activities in your free time? Which ones?

What games are popular in your country? Describe how to play one.

외출 장소

박물관	1	museum
화랑	2	art gallery
음악회	3	concert
연극	4	play
놀이 공원	5	amusement park
유적지	6	historic site
국립 공원	7	national park

수공예 전시회	8	craft fair
알뜰시장	9	yard sale
중고품 교환 시장	10	swap meet/
벼룩 시장		flea market
공원	11	park
해변	12	beach
산	13	mountains

수족관	14	aquarium
식물원	15	botanical gardens
별자리 투영관	16	planetarium
동물원	17	zoo
영화	18	movies
이동 유원지	19	carnival
축제장	20	fair

A. What do you want to do today?
B. Let's go to { a/an ___[1–9]___.
              the ___[10–20]___

A. What did you do over the weekend?
B. I went to { a/an ___[1–9]___.
             the ___[10–20]___

A. What are you going to do on your day off?
B. I'm going to go to { a/an ___[1–9]___.
                      the ___[10–20]___

What are some of your favorite places to go? Where are they? What do you do there?

공원과 놀이터

자전거 전용도로	**1**	bicycle path/ bike path/ bikeway	조깅로	**8**	jogging path	놀이터	**16**	playground
연못	**2**	duck pond	벤치	**9**	bench	클라이밍 월 (등반연습용 벽)	**17**	climbing wall
피크닉 구역	**3**	picnic area	테니스 코트	**10**	tennis court	그네	**18**	swings
쓰레기통	**4**	trash can	소프트볼 구장	**11**	ballfield	등반 놀이기	**19**	climber
석쇠판	**5**	grill	분수	**12**	fountain	미끄럼틀	**20**	slide
피크닉 테이블	**6**	picnic table	자전거 보관대	**13**	bike rack	시소	**21**	seesaw
급수대	**7**	water fountain	회전목마	**14**	merry-go-round/ carousel	모래 놀이통	**22**	sandbox
			스케이트 보딩 경사로	**15**	skateboard ramp	모래	**23**	sand

[1–22]
A. Excuse me. Does this park
   have (a) _____?
B. Yes. Right over there.

[17–23]
A. { Be careful on the ____[17–21]____!
    { Be careful in the ____[22, 23]____!
B. I will, Dad/Mom.

Describe a park and playground you are familiar with.

해변

구조원	**1**	lifeguard	비치 의자	**10**	beach chair	냉각기(아이스 박스)	**21**	cooler
구조원 스탠드	**2**	lifeguard stand	비치 파라솔	**11**	beach umbrella	햇볕 모자	**22**	sun hat
구명 기구	**3**	life preserver	모래성	**12**	sand castle	자외선 차단제	**23**	sunscreen/
매점	**4**	snack bar/	서프보드(소형)	**13**	boogie board			sunblock/
		refreshment	일광욕하는 사람	**14**	sunbather			suntan
		stand	선글라스/색안경	**15**	sunglasses			lotion
행상인	**5**	vendor	(비치) 타올	**16**	(beach) towel	비치 깔개 담요	**24**	(beach)
수영하는 사람	**6**	swimmer	비치볼	**17**	beach ball			blanket
파도	**7**	wave	서프보드	**18**	surfboard	삽	**25**	shovel
파도타기하는 사람	**8**	surfer	조개껍질	**19**	seashell/shell	양동이	**26**	pail
연	**9**	kite	돌	**20**	rock			

[1–26]
A. What a nice beach!
B. It is. Look at all the _____s!

[9–11, 13, 15–18, 21–26]
A. Are you ready for the beach?
B. Almost. I just have to get my _____.

Do you like to go to the beach? Describe your favorite beach. What do you take when you go there?

야외 레크레이션

캠핑/야영	**A**	**camping**
텐트/천막	**1**	tent
침낭	**2**	sleeping bag
말뚝	**3**	tent stakes
랜턴	**4**	lantern
손도끼/도끼	**5**	hatchet
캠핑 스토브	**6**	camping stove
다용도 나이프	**7**	Swiss army knife
해충약	**8**	insect repellent
성냥	**9**	matches

하이킹	**B**	**hiking**
배낭	**10**	backpack
수통	**11**	canteen
나침판	**12**	compass
지도	**13**	trail map
위치 확인 시스템 장치	**14**	GPS device
등산화	**15**	hiking boots

암벽 등반/ 전문 등반	**C**	**rock climbing/ technical climbing**
등산 멜빵	**16**	harness
로프/등산용 밧줄	**17**	rope

산악 자전거 타기	**D**	**mountain biking**
산악 자전거	**18**	mountain bike
(자전거) 헬멧	**19**	(bike) helmet

야유회	**E**	**picnic**
(피크닉) 깔개 담요	**20**	(picnic) blanket
보온병	**21**	thermos
피크닉 바구니	**22**	picnic basket

A. Let's go __[A–E]__ * this weekend.
B. Good idea! We haven't gone __[A–E]__ * in a long time.

*With E, say: on a picnic.

A. Did you bring
 { the __[1–9, 11–14, 16, 17, 20–22]__ ?
 { your __[10, 15, 18, 19]__ ?
B. Yes, I did.
A. Oh, good.

Have you ever gone camping, hiking, rock climbing, or mountain biking? Tell about it: What did you do? Where? What equipment did you use?

Do you like to go on picnics? Where? What picnic supplies and food do you take with you?

개인 스포츠 및 레크레이션

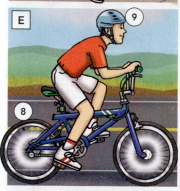

조깅	**A jogging**
조깅복	**1** jogging suit
조깅화	**2** jogging shoes
육상	**B running**
육상용 반바지/육상복	**3** running shorts
육상화	**4** running shoes
걷기	**C walking**
운동화	**5** walking shoes
인라인 스케이팅/롤러 스케이팅	**D inline skating/rollerblading**
인라인 스케이트화/롤러브레이드	**6** inline skates/rollerblades
무릎 보호대	**7** knee pads
싸이클링	**E cycling/biking**
자전거	**8** bicycle/bike
(자전거) 헬멧	**9** (bicycle/bike) helmet
스케이트 보딩	**F skateboarding**
스케이트 보드	**10** skateboard
팔꿈치 보호대	**11** elbow pads
볼링	**G bowling**
볼링 볼	**12** bowling ball
볼링화	**13** bowling shoes

승마	**H horseback riding**
안장	**14** saddle
고삐	**15** reins
등자(말 안장에 달린)	**16** stirrups
테니스	**I tennis**
테니스 라켓	**17** tennis racket
테니스 공	**18** tennis ball
테니스 반바지	**19** tennis shorts
배드민턴	**J badminton**
배드민턴 라켓	**20** badminton racket
깃털공 (베드민턴의)	**21** birdie/shuttlecock
라켓볼	**K racquetball**
보호 안경	**22** safety goggles
라켓볼	**23** racquetball
라켓	**24** racquet
탁구	**L table tennis/ ping pong**
탁구채	**25** paddle
탁구대	**26** ping pong table
네트	**27** net
탁구공	**28** ping pong ball

골프	**M**	**golf**	체조	**Q**	**gymnastics**	권투	**T**	**box**
골프채	**29**	golf clubs	안마	**36**	horse	권투 글러브	**45**	boxing gloves
골프공	**30**	golf ball	이단 평행봉	**37**	parallel bars	복싱 팬티	**46**	(boxing) trunks
			매트	**38**	mat			
프리스비	**N**	**Frisbee**	평균대	**39**	balance beam	레슬링	**U**	**wrestle**
프리스비/	**31**	Frisbee/	트램펄린	**40**	trampoline	레슬링복	**47**	wrestling uniform
원반 던지기		flying disc				(레슬링) 매트	**48**	(wrestling) mat
			역도	**R**	**weightlifting**			
당구	**O**	**billiards/pool**	바벨	**41**	barbell	헬스 운동	**V**	**work out/exercise**
당구대	**32**	pool table	역기	**42**	weights	트레드밀	**49**	treadmill
당구채	**33**	pool stick				로잉 머신	**50**	rowing machine
당구공	**34**	billiard balls	궁도	**S**	**archery**	(노젓기 연습 기구)		
			활과 화살	**43**	bow and arrow	실내 운동용 자전거	**51**	exercise bike
격투기	**P**	**martial arts**	과녁	**44**	target	만능운동기구	**52**	universal/
검은띠	**35**	black belt						exercise equipment

[A–V]
A. What do you like to do in your free time?
B. { I like to go ___[A–H]___ .
I like to play ___[I–O]___ .
I like to do ___[P–S]___ .
I like to ___[T–V]___ .

[1–52]
A. I really like this / these new _____ .
B. It's / They're very nice.

Do you do any of these activities? Which ones? Which are popular in your country?

TEAM SPORTS

단체 스포츠

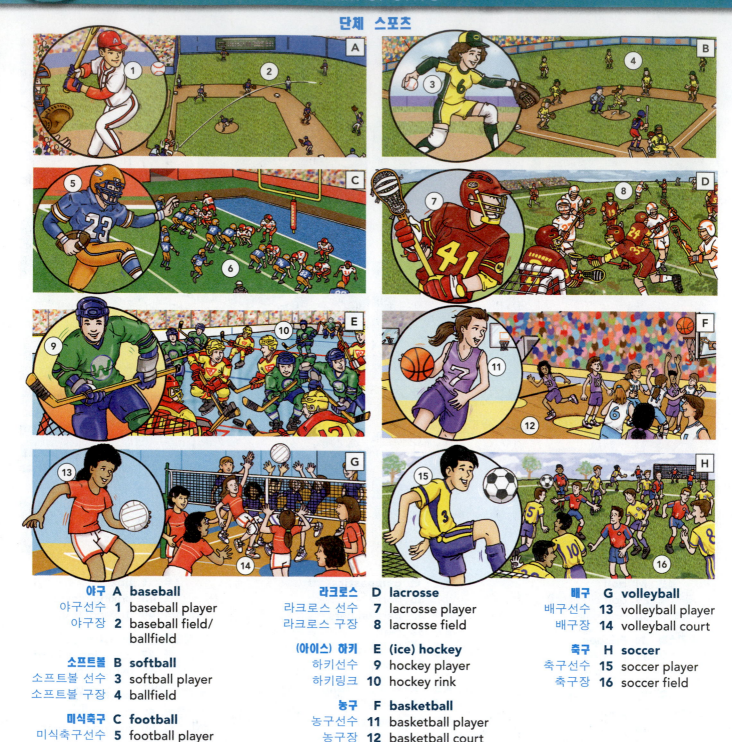

	야구	**A**	**baseball**
야구선수		**1**	baseball player
야구장		**2**	baseball field/ballfield

	소프트볼	**B**	**softball**
소프트볼 선수		**3**	softball player
소프트볼 구장		**4**	ballfield

	미식축구	**C**	**football**
미식축구선수		**5**	football player
미식축구장		**6**	football field

	라크로스	**D**	**lacrosse**
라크로스 선수		**7**	lacrosse player
라크로스 구장		**8**	lacrosse field

	(아이스) 하키	**E**	**(ice) hockey**
하키선수		**9**	hockey player
하키링크		**10**	hockey rink

	농구	**F**	**basketball**
농구선수		**11**	basketball player
농구장		**12**	basketball court

	배구	**G**	**volleyball**
배구선수		**13**	volleyball player
배구장		**14**	volleyball court

	축구	**H**	**soccer**
축구선수		**15**	soccer player
축구장		**16**	soccer field

[A–H]
A. Do you like to play **baseball**?
B. Yes. **Baseball** is one of my favorite sports.

A. .... plays __[A–H]__ very well.
B. You're right. I think he's/she's one of the best _____s* on the team.

*Use 1, 3, 5, 7, 9, 11, 13, 15.

A. Now listen, team! I want all of you to go out on that _____† and play the best game of __[A–H]__ you've ever played!
B. All right, Coach!

† Use 2, 4, 6, 8, 10, 12, 14, 16.

Which sports in this lesson do you like to play? Which do you like to watch?

What are your favorite teams?

Name some famous players of these sports.

단체 스포츠 장비

야구/야구공	**A**	**baseball**
야구/야구공	1	baseball
배트/방망이	2	bat
타자수 헬멧	3	batting helmet
(야구)유니폼	4	(baseball) uniform
포수 마스크	5	catcher's mask
(야구) 글러브	6	(baseball) glove
포수 글러브	7	catcher's mitt

소프트볼	**B**	**softball**
소프트볼공	8	softball
소프트볼 글러브	9	softball glove

미식축구	**C**	**football**
미식축구공	10	football
미식축구 헬멧	11	football helmet
어깨 보호대/어깨패드	12	shoulder pads

라크로스	**D**	**lacrosse**
라크로스 볼	13	lacrosse ball
얼굴 가리개	14	face guard
라크로스 스틱	15	lacrosse stick

(아이스) 하키	**E**	**(ice) hockey**
하키퍽	16	hockey puck
하키 스틱	17	hockey stick
하키 마스크	18	hockey mask
하키 글러브	19	hockey glove
하키 스케이트	20	hockey skates

농구	**F**	**basketball**
농구공	21	basketball
백보드	22	backboard
농구 골인망	23	basketball hoop

배구	**G**	**volleyball**
배구공	24	volleyball
배구 네트	25	volleyball net

축구	**H**	**soccer**
축구공	26	soccer ball
정강이 보호대	27	shinguards

[1–27]
A. I can't find my **baseball**!
B. Look in the closet.*

*closet, basement, garage

[In a store]
A. Excuse me. I'm looking for (a) __[1–27]__ .
B. All our __[A–H]__ equipment is over there.
A. Thanks.

[At home]
A. I'm going to play __[A–H]__ after school today.
B. Don't forget your __[1–21, 24, 26, 27]__ !

Which sports in this lesson are popular in your country? Which sports do students play in high school?

겨울 스포츠와 레크레이션

(활강) 스키 A (downhill) skiing
스키 **1** skis
스키 부츠 **2** ski boots
바인딩 **3** bindings
(스키) 폴 **4** (ski) poles

크로스 컨트리 스키 B cross-country skiing
크로스 컨트리 스키 **5** cross-country skis

(아이스) 스케이팅 C (ice) skating
(아이스)스케이트 **6** (ice) skates
스케이트 날 **7** blade
스케이트날 집 **8** skate guard

피겨스케이팅 D figure skating
피겨스케이트 **9** figure skates

스노보드타기 E snowboarding
스노보드 **10** snowboard

썰매타기 F sledding
썰매 **11** sled
원반 눈썰매 **12** sledding dish/ saucer

봅슬레이 경주 G bobsledding
봅슬레이 **13** bobsled

설상차 경주/스노우모빌 H snowmobiling
설상차 **14** snowmobile

[A–H]
A. What's your favorite winter sport?
B. **Skiing.**

[A–H]
[At work or at school on Friday]
A. What are you going to do this weekend?
B. I'm going to go _____.

[1–14]
[On the telephone]
A. Hello. *Sally's* Sporting Goods.
B. Hello. Do you sell _____(s)?
A. Yes, we do. / No, we don't.

Have you ever done any of these activities? Which ones?

Have you ever watched the Winter Olympics? Which event do you think is the most exciting? the most dangerous?

수상 스포츠와 레크레이션

요트타기 A sailing	구명 조끼 **10** life jacket/ life vest	**파도타기 I surfing**
요트 **1** sailboat		서프보드 **20** surfboard
구명 조끼 **2** life jacket/life vest	**수영 F swimming**	
	수영복 **11** swimsuit/ bathing suit	**윈드서핑 J windsurfing**
카누경기 B canoeing		윈드 서프보드/세일보드 **21** sailboard
카누 **3** canoe	물안경 **12** goggles	돛 **22** sail
노 **4** paddles	수영모 **13** bathing cap	
		수상스키타기 K waterskiing
노젓기 C rowing	**잠수 G snorkeling**	수상스키 **23** water skis
노젓는 배 **5** rowboat	마스크 **14** mask	견인 밧줄 **24** towrope
노 **6** oars	잠수용 호흡관/스노클 **15** snorkel	
	물갈퀴 **16** fins	**낚시 L fishing**
카약 경기 D kayaking		(낚시용)대 **25** (fishing) rod/ pole
카약 **7** kayak	**스쿠버 다이빙 H scuba diving**	릴 **26** reel
노 **8** paddles	잠수복 **17** wet suit	(낚시용)줄 **27** (fishing) line
	(산소)탱크 **18** (air) tank	(낚시용)망 **28** (fishing) net
(급류)래프팅 E (white-water) rafting	(수중)마스크 **19** (diving) mask	미끼 **29** bait
고무 보트(래프팅 용) **9** raft		

[A–L]
A. Would you like to go **sailing** tomorrow?
B. Sure. I'd love to.

A. Have you ever gone [A–L] ?
B. Yes, I have./ No, I haven't.

A. Do you have everything you need to go [A–L] ?
B. Yes. I have my [1–29] (and my [1–29]).
A. Have a good time!

Which sports in this lesson have you tried? Which sports would you like to try?

Are any of these sports popular in your country? Which ones?

스포츠 및 운동 활동

치다	**1**	hit	숫을 하다	**10**	shoot
던지다	**2**	pitch	뻗다/펴다	**11**	stretch
던지다	**3**	throw	구부리다	**12**	bend
받다	**4**	catch	걷다	**13**	walk
패스하다	**5**	pass	달리다	**14**	run
차다	**6**	kick	깡충 뛰다	**15**	hop
서브하다	**7**	serve	가볍게 뛰다	**16**	skip
튀기다	**8**	bounce	점프하다	**17**	jump
드리블하다	**9**	dribble	뻗다	**18**	reach

휘두르다	**19**	swing	거수 도약 운동	**27**	jumping jack
들어 올리다	**20**	lift	재주넘기를 하다	**28**	somersault
수영하다	**21**	swim	옆으로 재주넘기를 하다	**29**	cartwheel
다이빙하다	**22**	dive	물구나무서기를 하다	**30**	handstand
쏘다	**23**	shoot			
엎드려팔굽혀펴기	**24**	push-up			
윗몸 일으키기	**25**	sit-up			
무릎굽히기	**26**	deep knee bend			

[1–10]
A. _____ the ball!
B. Okay, Coach!

[11–23]
A. Now _____!
B. Like this?
A. Yes.

[24–30]
A. Okay, everybody. I want you to do twenty _____s!
B. Twenty _____s?!
A. That's right.

Do you exercise regularly?
Which exercises do you do?

Be an exercise instructor! Lead your friends in an exercise routine using the actions in this lesson.

오락

연극	**A**	**play**
극장	**1**	theater
배우	**2**	actor
여자배우	**3**	actress
연주	**B**	**concert**
콘서트 홀/연주회장	**4**	concert hall
관현악단/오케스트라	**5**	orchestra
음악가	**6**	musician
지휘자	**7**	conductor
악단	**8**	band

오페라	**C**	**opera**
오페라 가수	**9**	opera singer
발레	**D**	**ballet**
발레댄서	**10**	ballet dancer
발레리나/	**11**	ballerina
여자무용수		
음악 클럽	**E**	**music club**
가수	**12**	singer

영화	**F**	**movies**
(영화)극장	**13**	(movie) theater
영사막	**14**	(movie) screen
여자 배우	**15**	actress
남자 배우	**16**	actor
코미디 클럽	**G**	**comedy club**
코미디언	**17**	comedian

[A–G]
A. What are you doing this evening?
B. I'm going to { a _____ [A, B, E, G].
the _____ [C, D, F].

[1–17]
A. What a magnificent _____!
B. I agree.

What kinds of entertainment in this lesson do you like?
What kinds of entertainment are popular in your country?

Who are some of your favorite actors? actresses?
musicians? singers? comedians?

오락 종류

A

B

음악	**A**	**music**	랩음악	**6**	rap music	연극	**B**	**plays**
고전음악	**1**	classical music	복음 성가	**7**	gospel music	드라마	**13**	drama
대중음악	**2**	popular music	재즈	**8**	jazz	코미디	**14**	comedy
컨츄리음악	**3**	country music	블루스	**9**	blues	비극	**15**	tragedy
록음악	**4**	rock music	블루그래스	**10**	bluegrass	희가극/뮤지컬	**16**	musical
민속음악	**5**	folk music	힙합	**11**	hip hop			(comedy)
			레게음악	**12**	reggae			

영화	C	movies/films
드라마	17	drama
코미디	18	comedy
서부영화	19	western
미스테리	20	mystery
뮤지컬	21	musical
만화영화	22	cartoon
다큐멘터리	23	documentary
액션영화	24	action movie/ adventure movie
전쟁영화	25	war movie

공포영화	26	horror movie
공상과학영화	27	science fiction movie
외국영화	28	foreign film

텔레비전 프로그램	D	TV programs
드라마	29	drama
시츄에이션 코미디/ 시트콤	30	(situation) comedy/ sitcom
토크쇼	31	talk show
게임 쇼/ 퀴즈쇼	32	game show/ quiz show

실제 체험쇼	33	reality show
연속 멜로 드라마	34	soap opera
만화영화	35	cartoon
어린이 프로	36	children's program
뉴스 프로	37	news program
스포츠 프로	38	sports program
자연계	39	nature program
다큐멘터리 프로 쇼핑 프로	40	shopping program

A. What kind of ___[A–D]___ do you like?
B. { I like ___[1–12]___ .
    { I like ___[13–40]___ s.

What's your favorite type of music?
Who is your favorite singer? musician?
musical group?

What kind of movies do you like?
Who are your favorite movie stars?
What are the titles of your favorite movies?

What kind of TV programs do you like?
What are your favorite shows?

악기

현악기	Strings
바이올린	**1** violin
비올라	**2** viola
첼로	**3** cello
콘트라베이스	**4** bass
기타	**5** (acoustic) guitar
전자기타	**6** electric guitar
밴조	**7** banjo
하프	**8** harp

목관악기	Woodwinds
피콜로	**9** piccolo
플루트	**10** flute
클라리넷	**11** clarinet

오보에	**12** oboe
리코더	**13** recorder
색소폰	**14** saxophone
파곳/바순	**15** bassoon

금관악기	Brass
트럼펫	**16** trumpet
트럼본	**17** trombone
프렌치 혼	**18** French horn
튜바	**19** tuba

타악기	Percussion
드럼	**20** drums
심벌즈	**a** cymbals

탬버린	**21** tambourine
실로폰	**22** xylophone

건반악기	Keyboard Instruments
피아노	**23** piano
전자 키보드	**24** electric keyboard
오르간	**25** organ

기타 악기	Other Instruments
아코디언	**26** accordion
하모니카	**27** harmonica

A. Do you play a musical instrument?
B. Yes. I play the **violin**.

A. You play the **trumpet** very well.
B. Thank you.

A. What's that noise?!
B. That's my son/daughter practicing the **drums**.

Do you play a musical instrument? Which one?

Which instruments are usually in an orchestra? a marching band? a rock group?

Name and describe typical musical instruments in your country.

농장과 농장 동물

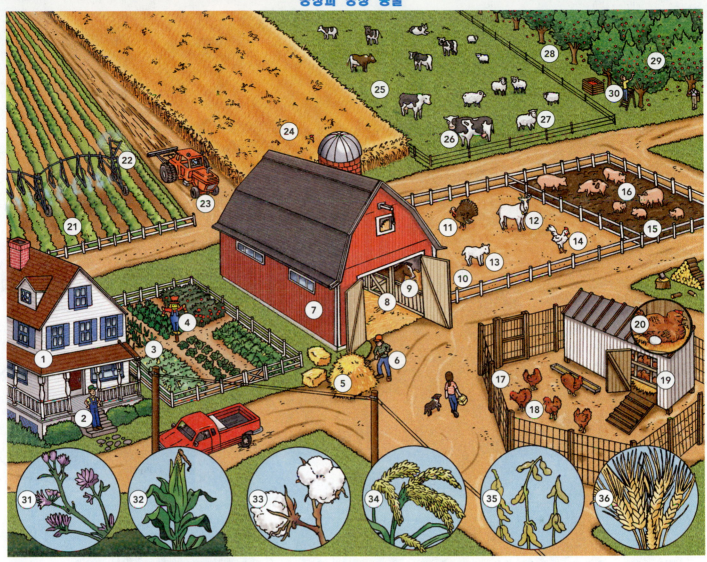

농가	**1** farmhouse	새끼양	**13** lamb	목초지	**25** pasture
농장주	**2** farmer	수탉	**14** rooster	젖소	**26** cow
텃밭	**3** (vegetable) garden	돼지우리	**15** pig pen	양	**27** sheep
허수아비	**4** scarecrow	돼지	**16** pig	과수원	**28** orchard
건초	**5** hay	닭장	**17** chicken coop	과수	**29** fruit tree
품꾼	**6** hired hand	닭	**18** chicken	농장 일꾼	**30** farm worker
헛간	**7** barn	계사	**19** hen house	자주개자리	**31** alfalfa
외양간/마구간	**8** stable	암탉	**20** hen	옥수수	**32** corn
말	**9** horse	농작물	**21** crop	목화	**33** cotton
헛간 앞마당	**10** barnyard	관개시설	**22** irrigation system	벼	**34** rice
칠면조	**11** turkey	트랙터	**23** tractor	콩	**35** soybeans
염소	**12** goat	밭/논/들판	**24** field	밀	**36** wheat

[1–30]
A. Where's the _____?
B. In / Next to the _____.

A. The [9, 11–14, 16, 18, 20, 26] s / [27] are loose again!
B. Oh, no! Where are they?
A. They're in the [1, 3, 7, 8, 10, 15, 17, 19, 24, 25, 28].

[31–36]
A. Do you grow _____ on your farm?
B. No. We grow _____.

Tell about farms in your country. What crops and animals are common on these farms?

동물과 애완동물

무스	**1** moose	여우	**10** fox	아르마딜로	**20** armadillo	프레리도그	**33** prairie dog
뿔	**a** antler	스컹크	**11** skunk	박쥐	**21** bat	고양이	**34** cat
북극곰	**2** polar bear	고슴도치	**12** porcupine	지렁이	**22** worm	수염	**a** whiskers
사슴	**3** deer	침(고슴도치	**a** quill	민달팽이	**23** slug	새끼고양이	**35** kitten
발굽-발굽들	**a** hoof-hooves	등의)		원숭이	**24** monkey	개	**36** dog
늑대-늑대들	**4** wolf-wolves	토끼	**13** rabbit	개미핥기	**25** anteater	강아지	**37** puppy
(짐승의) 모피/털	**a** coat/fur	비버	**14** beaver	라마	**26** llama	햄스터	**38** hamster
(흑)곰	**5** (black) bear	너구리	**15** raccoon	재규어	**27** jaguar	애완용쥐	**39** gerbil
갈고리 발톱	**a** claw	주머니쥐	**16** possum/	반점	**a** spots	돼지쥐	**40** guinea pig
쿠거	**6** mountain lion		opossum	생쥐	**28** mouse-mice	금붕어	**41** goldfish
(회색)곰	**7** (grizzly) bear	말	**17** horse	쥐	**29** rat	카나리아	**42** canary
버팔로/들소	**8** buffalo/bison	꼬리	**a** tail	칩멍크	**30** chipmunk	잉꼬	**43** parakeet
코요테	**9** coyote	조랑말	**18** pony	다람쥐	**31** squirrel		
		당나귀	**19** donkey	땅다람쥐	**32** gopher		

영양	**44** antelope	호랑이	**51** tiger	하이에나	**54** hyena	표범	**60** leopard
비비	**45** baboon	동물의 발	**a** paw	사자	**55** lion	고릴라	**61** gorilla
코뿔소	**46** rhinoceros	낙타	**52** camel	갈기	**a** mane	캥거루	**62** kangaroo
뿔(소, 양 등의)	**a** horn	혹(낙타 등의)	**a** hump	기린	**56** giraffe	육아주머니	**a** pouch
팬더	**47** panda	코끼리	**53** elephant	얼룩말	**57** zebra	코알라	**63** koala (bear)
오랑우탄	**48** orangutan	엄니	**a** tusk	줄무늬	**a** stripes	오리너구리	**64** platypus
표범	**49** panther	(코끼리 등의)		침팬지	**58** chimpanzee		
긴팔원숭이	**50** gibbon	코끼리 코	**b** trunk	하마	**59** hippopotamus		

[1–33, 44–64]
A. Look at that _____!
B. Wow! That's the biggest _____ I've ever seen!

[34–43]
A. Do you have a pet?
B. Yes. I have a _____.
A. What's your _____'s name?
B. ....

What animals are there where you live?

Is there a zoo near where you live? What animals does it have?

What are some common pets in your country?

If you could be an animal, which animal would you like to be? Why?

Does your culture have any popular folk tales or children's stories about animals? Tell a story you know.

새와 곤충

조류	**Birds**						
울새	**1** robin	매	**9** hawk	앵무새	**22** parrot	거미	**33** spider
둥지	**a** nest	독수리	**10** eagle	타조	**23** ostrich	거미줄	**a** web
알	**b** egg	발톱	**a** claw			사마귀	**34** praying mantis
큰어치	**2** blue jay	백조	**11** swan	곤충	**Insects**		
날개	**a** wing	벌새	**12** hummingbird	파리	**24** fly	말벌	**35** wasp
꼬리	**b** tail	오리	**13** duck	무당벌레	**25** ladybug	꿀벌	**36** bee
깃털	**c** feather	부리	**a** bill	개똥벌레	**26** firefly/ lightning bug	벌집	**a** beehive
홍관조	**3** cardinal	참새	**14** sparrow			메뚜기	**37** grasshopper
까마귀	**4** crow	거위	**15** goose-geese	나방	**27** moth	딱정벌레	**38** beetle
갈매기	**5** seagull	펭귄	**16** penguin	애벌레	**28** caterpillar	전갈	**39** scorpion
딱따구리	**6** woodpecker	홍학	**17** flamingo	고치	**a** cocoon	지네	**40** centipede
부리	**a** beak	두루미	**18** crane	나비	**29** butterfly	귀뚜라미	**41** cricket
비둘기	**7** pigeon	황새	**19** stork	진드기	**30** tick		
부엉이	**8** owl	펠리컨	**20** pelican	모기	**31** mosquito		
		공작	**21** peacock	잠자리	**32** dragonfly		

[1–41]
A. Is that a/an _____?
B. No. I think it's a/an _____.

[24–41]
A. Hold still! There's a _____ on your shirt!
B. Oh! Can you get it off me?
A. There! It's gone!

What birds and insects are there where you live?

Does your culture have any popular folk tales or children's stories about birds or insects? Tell a story you know.

생선, 바다 동물 및 파충류

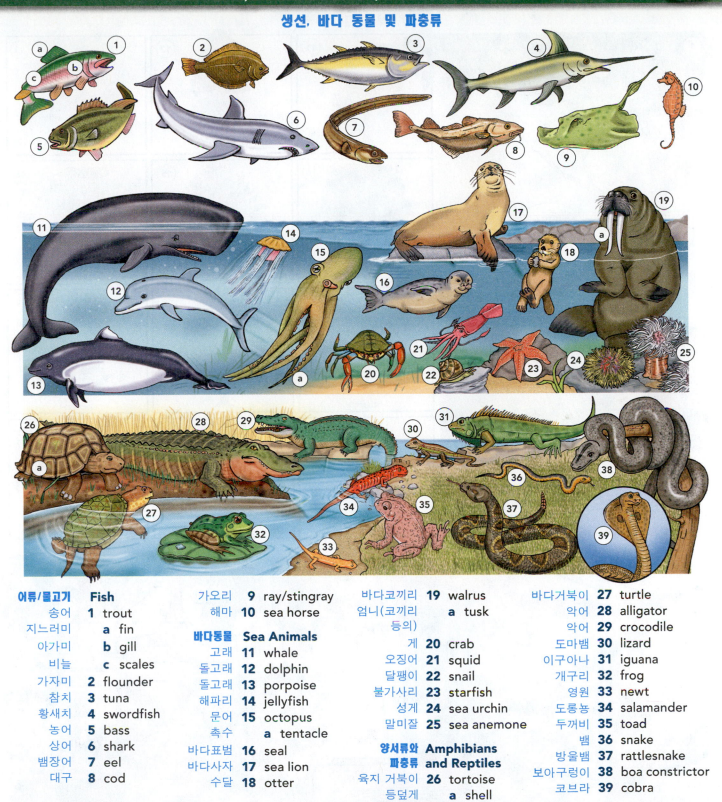

어류/물고기	**Fish**
송어	**1** trout
지느러미	**a** fin
아가미	**b** gill
비늘	**c** scales
가자미	**2** flounder
참치	**3** tuna
황새치	**4** swordfish
농어	**5** bass
상어	**6** shark
뱀장어	**7** eel
대구	**8** cod

가오리	**9** ray/stingray
해마	**10** sea horse
바다동물	**Sea Animals**
고래	**11** whale
돌고래	**12** dolphin
돌고래	**13** porpoise
해파리	**14** jellyfish
문어	**15** octopus
촉수	**a** tentacle
바다표범	**16** seal
바다사자	**17** sea lion
수달	**18** otter

바다코끼리	**19** walrus
엄니(코끼리 등의)	**a** tusk
게	**20** crab
오징어	**21** squid
달팽이	**22** snail
불가사리	**23** starfish
성게	**24** sea urchin
말미잘	**25** sea anemone
양서류와 파충류	**Amphibians and Reptiles**
육지 거북이	**26** tortoise
등딱게	**a** shell

바다거북이	**27** turtle
악어	**28** alligator
악어	**29** crocodile
도마뱀	**30** lizard
이구아나	**31** iguana
개구리	**32** frog
영원	**33** newt
도롱뇽	**34** salamander
두꺼비	**35** toad
뱀	**36** snake
방울뱀	**37** rattlesnake
보아구렁이	**38** boa constrictor
코브라	**39** cobra

[1–39]
A. Is that a/an _____?
B. No. I think it's a/an _____.

[26–39]
A. Are there any _____s around here?
B. No. But there are lots of _____!

What fish, sea animals, and reptiles can be found in your country? Which ones are endangered and need to be protected? Why?

In your opinion, which ones are the most interesting? the most beautiful? the most dangerous?

나무, 식물 그리고 꽃

나무	1	tree	솔방울	10	pine cone	참나무	19	oak	고비	27	fern
나뭇잎	2	leaf-leaves	층층나무	11	dogwood	소나무	20	pine	초목	28	plant
잔가지	3	twig	호랑가시나무	12	holly	미국 삼나무	21	redwood	선인장-	29	cactus-cacti
가지	4	branch	목련	13	magnolia	버드나무	22	(weeping)	선인장들		
큰가지	5	limb	느릅나무	14	elm			willow	덩굴	30	vine
줄기	6	trunk	벗나무	15	cherry	떨기나무	23	bush	덩굴 옻나무	31	poison ivy
나무껍질	7	bark	야자수	16	palm	호랑가시나무	24	holly	옻나무	32	poison sumac
뿌리	8	root	자작나무	17	birch	딸기류 열매	25	berries	떡갈 옻나무	33	poison oak
침엽	9	needle	단풍나무	18	maple	관목	26	shrub			

꽃 **34** flower	천수국 **43** marigold	해바라기 **52** sunflower
꽃잎 **35** petal	카네이션 **44** carnation	크로커스 **53** crocus
줄기 **36** stem	치자나무 **45** gardenia	튤립 **54** tulip
꽃봉오리 **37** bud	백합 **46** lily	제라늄 **55** geranium
가시 **38** thorn	붓꽃 **47** iris	제비꽃 **56** violet
알뿌리 **39** bulb	팬지 **48** pansy	홍성초 **57** poinsettia
국화 **40** chrysanthemum	페튜니아 **49** petunia	재스민 **58** jasmine
나팔수선화 **41** daffodil	난초 **50** orchid	불상화 **59** hibiscus
데이지 **42** daisy	장미 **51** rose	

[11–22]
A. What kind of tree is that?
B. I think it's a/an _____ tree.

[31–33]
A. Watch out for the _____ over there!
B. Oh. Thanks for the warning.

[40–57]
A. Look at all the _____s!*
B. They're beautiful!

*With 58 and 59, use: Look at all the ___!

Describe your favorite tree and your favorite flower.

What kinds of trees and flowers grow where you live?

In your country, what flowers do you see at weddings? at funerals? during holidays? in hospital rooms? Tell which flowers people use for different occasions.

에너지, 자연보호 및 환경

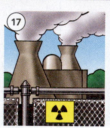

에너지 자원	**Sources of Energy**	자연보호	**Conservation**	환경문제	**Environmental Problems**
석유	**1** oil/petroleum	재활용하다	**9** recycle	공기오염	**13** air pollution
(천연) 가스	**2** (natural) gas	에너지를 절약하다	**10** save energy/ conserve energy	수질오염	**14** water pollution
석탄	**3** coal			유해 폐기물	**15** hazardous waste/ toxic waste
원자력에너지/핵에너지	**4** nuclear energy	물을 절약하다	**11** save water/ conserve water		
태양에너지	**5** solar energy			산성비	**16** acid rain
수력 발전	**6** hydroelectric power	카풀	**12** carpool	방사선	**17** radiation
바람	**7** wind			지구 온난화	**18** global warming
지열에너지	**8** geothermal energy				

[1–8]
A. In my opinion, _____ will be our best source of energy in the future.
B. I disagree. I think our best source of energy will be _____.

[9–12]
A. Do you _____?
B. Yes. I'm very concerned about the environment.

[13–18]
A. Do you worry about the environment?
B. Yes. I'm very concerned about _____.

What kind of energy do you use to heat your home? to cook? In your opinion, which will be the best source of energy in the future?

Do you practice conservation? What do you do to help the environment?

In your opinion, what is the most serious environmental problem in the world today? Why?

자연 재앙

지진	**1** earthquake	홍수	**6** flood	산사태	**11** landslide
허리케인	**2** hurricane	해일	**7** tsunami	이류	**12** mudslide
태풍	**3** typhoon	가뭄	**8** drought	눈사태	**13** avalanche
폭풍설	**4** blizzard	산불	**9** forest fire	화산 폭발	**14** volcanic eruption
토네이도	**5** tornado	자연 화재	**10** wildfire		

A. Did you hear about the _____ in ......(country)......?
B. Yes, I did. I saw it on the news.

Have you or someone you know ever experienced a natural disaster? Tell about it.

Which natural disasters sometimes happen where you live? How do people prepare for them?

여행 종류

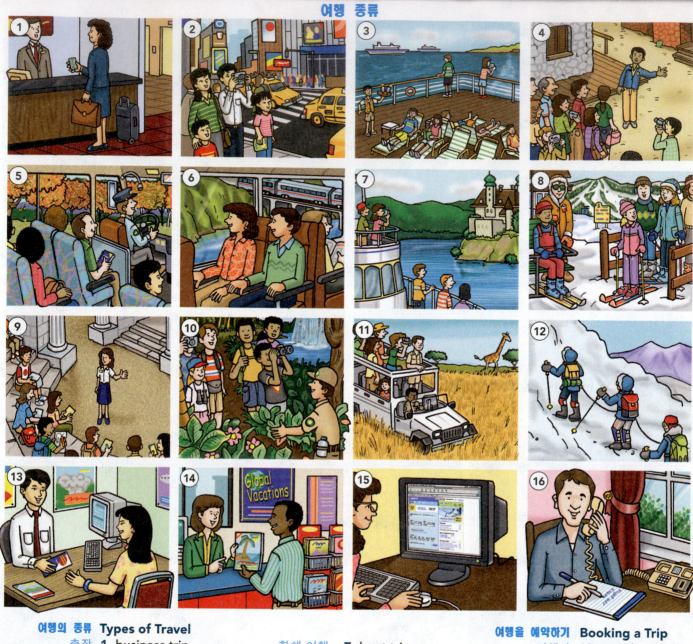

여행의 종류 Types of Travel

출장	**1**	business trip
가족 여행	**2**	family trip
순항	**3**	cruise
가이드 딸린 여행	**4**	(guided) tour
버스 여행	**5**	bus tour
기차 여행	**6**	train trip
항해 여행	**7**	boat trip
스키 여행	**8**	ski trip
학습 여행	**9**	study tour
생태보호 여행	**10**	eco-tour
사파리 여행	**11**	safari
원정	**12**	expedition

여행을 예약하기 Booking a Trip

여행사	**13**	travel agency
투어 전문 여행사	**14**	tour company
온라인으로	**15**	online
전화를 통하여	**16**	over the phone

[1–12]
A. Are you planning to travel soon?
B. Yes. I'm going on a _____ to ..(country)..
A. A _____ to ..(country)..? That's wonderful!

[13–16]
A. How did you make the arrangements for your trip?
B. I booked it { through a ____[13, 14]____.
  ____[15, 16]____

Tell about a trip you took: Where did you travel? What kind of trip was it? How did you book the trip?

목적지에 도착

입국 심사	**1** immigration/passport control		호텔 특별 차량	**8** hotel courtesy vehicles
수화물 회수장	**2** baggage claim area		화장실	**9** restrooms
세관	**3** customs		여권	**10** passport
환전 카운터	**4** money exchange counter		비자	**11** visa
택시 승차장	**5** taxi stand		수화물 회수표	**12** baggage claim check
셔틀 버스	**6** shuttle bus		세관 신고서	**13** customs declaration form
자동차 렌트 카운터	**7** car rental counters			

[1–9]

A. Excuse me. { Where's ____[1, 3]____ ?
Where's the ____[2, 4–6]____ ?
Where are the ____[7–9]____ ?

B. Over there.

[10–13]

A. May I see your _____?
B. My _____? Yes. Here you are.
A. Thank you.

[At immigration/passport control]

A. What is the purpose of your trip—business or pleasure?

B. ....

A. How long do you plan to stay?

B. ....

[At customs]

A. How many bags do you have?

B. ....

A. Can you open them, please?
I need to inspect them.

B. Certainly.

Tell about your arrival at a destination:

Where did you arrive?
What happened after you arrived?
Where did you go?
What did you do?

호텔 커뮤니케이션

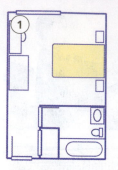

1인실	**1**	single room
더블베드 2인실	**2**	room with double beds
비흡연실	**3**	non-smoking room
장애인 전용실	**4**	handicapped-accessible room
전망 있는 방	**5**	room with a view
스위트룸	**6**	suite
룸서비스	**7**	Room Service
객실 관리	**8**	Housekeeping
보수 관리	**9**	Maintenance
프런트	**10**	Front Desk

호텔 안내 접수계	**11**	Concierge
벨 데스크	**12**	Bell Desk
저녁을 주문하고 싶습니다.	**a**	I'd like to order dinner.
타월이 몇 벌 필요합니다.	**b**	We need some towels.
우리 방의 세면기가 고장 났습니다.	**c**	The sink in our room is broken.
아침 7시에 모닝 콜을 좀 해주세요.	**d**	I'd like a wake-up call at 7 a.m., please.
쇼 티켓을 구하고 싶습니다.	**e**	I'd like to get tickets for a show.
체크 아웃을 하려고 합니다. 짐을 들어줄 사람을 좀 보내주겠습니까?	**f**	I'm checking out. Can you please send someone to get my bags?

[1–6]
A. I'd like a _____, please.
B. Let me see if that's available.
A. Thank you.

A. ___[7–12]___.
B. ___[a–f]___.
A. Certainly.

Tell about a hotel you stayed in: What type of room did you have? What hotel services did you use?

관광객 활동

Table for two at 7:00?

관광하러 가다	**1**	go sightseeing
도보 투어를 하다	**2**	take a walking tour
버스 투어를 하다	**3**	take a bus tour
환전하다	**4**	exchange money
기념품을 사다	**5**	buy souvenirs
엽서들을 부치다	**6**	mail some postcards

식당 예약을 하다	**7**	make a restaurant reservation
자동차를 렌트하다	**8**	rent a car
쇼/연주회 티켓을 구하다	**9**	get tickets for a *show/concert*
유적지를 방문하다	**10**	visit an historic site
쇼핑하러 가다	**11**	go shopping

공원에 가다	**12**	go to a park
박물관에 가다	**13**	go to a museum
헬스클럽/ 체력단련실에 가다	**14**	go to a health club/fitness club
인터넷 카페에 가다	**15**	go to an Internet cafe
클럽에 가다	**16**	go to a club

A. May I help you?
B. Yes, please. I'd like to _____.

A. What did you do today?
B. We _____ed.

Tell about a tourist experience you had: Where did you go? What did you do there?

관광객 커뮤니케이션

Tourist Requests 여행객의 요청

Asking Permission 허락 받기

Talking with Local People 현지인과 이야기하기

a **Where are you from?** (11)

b **How long are you here for?** (12)

c **What have you seen?** (13)

d **How do you like our city?** (14)

환전하다 **1** exchange money
여행자 수표를 현금으로 바꾸다 **2** cash a traveler's check
이것을 사다 **3** buy this
티켓 두장을 사다 **4** buy two tickets
이것을 우리 나라에 부치다 **5** mail this to my country
여기서 사진을 찍다 **6** take photographs here
여기서 먹다 **7** eat here
들어가다 **8** go in

여기서 휴대폰을 사용하다. **9** use a cell phone here
신용 카드로 지불하다. **10** pay with a credit card
나는… 에서 왔습니다. **11** I'm from .....(country).....
여기에 5일 동안 머물 것입니다. **12** I'm here for five days.
제가 본 것은…과 … 입니다. **13** I've seen .... and ....
저는 당신의 도시가 아주 좋습니다.
이곳은 아주… 합니다. **14** I like your city very much. It's very ....

[1–5]
A. May I help you?
B. Yes, please. I'd like to _____.

[6–10]
A. Can I _____?
B. { Yes, you can.
     No, you can't.

[11–14]
A. ___[a–d]___?
B. ___[11–14]___.

Emergency Expressions 비상사태 표현

Useful Expressions 유용한 표현들

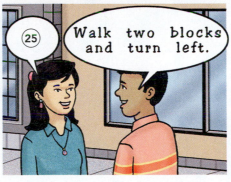

도와 주세요!	**15** Help!
경찰관!	**16** Police!
귀찮게 하지 마세요!/	**17** Please don't bother me!/
저리 가세요!/	Please go away!/
비켜요!	Get away from me!
불이야!	**18** Fire!
조심하세요!	**19** Look out!
꼼짝 마!	**20** Freeze!/Stop!/Don't move!

(언어)를 하십니까?	**21** Do you speak (language)?
그걸 좀 적어 주세요.	**22** Please write that down for me.
저것을 영어로 뭐라고 하지요?	**23** What do you call that in English?
그것을 다시 얘기해주세요.	**24** Please repeat that.
천천히 좀 얘기해주세요.	**25** Please speak slowly.
미안합니다.	**26** I'm sorry.
뭐라고 하셨죠?	What did you say?

Be a tourist! Practice conversations with other students. Use all the expressions on pages 164 and 165.

세계

ARCTIC OCEAN

Baffin Bay

GREENLAND

ICELAND

Hudson Bay

Bering Sea

ALEUTIAN ISLANDS

CANADA

NORTH AMERICA

ATLANTIC OCEAN

AZORES (Portugal)

UNITED STATES OF AMERICA

MOROCCO

CANARY ISLANDS (Spain)

WESTERN SAHARA

BERMUDA

HAWAIIAN ISLANDS (US)

MEXICO

Gulf of Mexico

THE BAHAMAS

CUBA

DOMINICAN REPUBLIC

JAMAICA

BELIZE

PUERTO RICO

SENEGAL

MAURITANIA

PACIFIC OCEAN

HONDURAS

HAITI

CAPE VERDE

GUATEMALA

NICARAGUA

GAMBIA

BURKINA FASO

EL SALVADOR

GUINEA-BISSAU

GUINEA

COSTA RICA

VENEZUELA

GUYANA

SURINAME

SIERRA LEONE

COTE D'IVOIRE

PANAMA

COLOMBIA

FRENCH GUIANA

LIBERIA

GHANA

PHOENIX ISLANDS

LINE ISLANDS

Equator

GALÁPAGOS ISLANDS

ECUADOR

EQUATORIAL GUINEA

KIRIBATI

AMERICAN SAMOA

PERU

SOUTH AMERICA

COOK ISLANDS

MARQUESAS ISLANDS

BRAZIL

WESTERN SAMOA

BOLIVIA

TAHITI

FRENCH POLYNESIA

PARAGUAY

TONGA

SOCIETY ISLANDS

CHILE

AUSTRAL ISLANDS

ARGENTINA

URUGUAY

N

W E

S

FALKLAND/MALVINAS ISLANDS

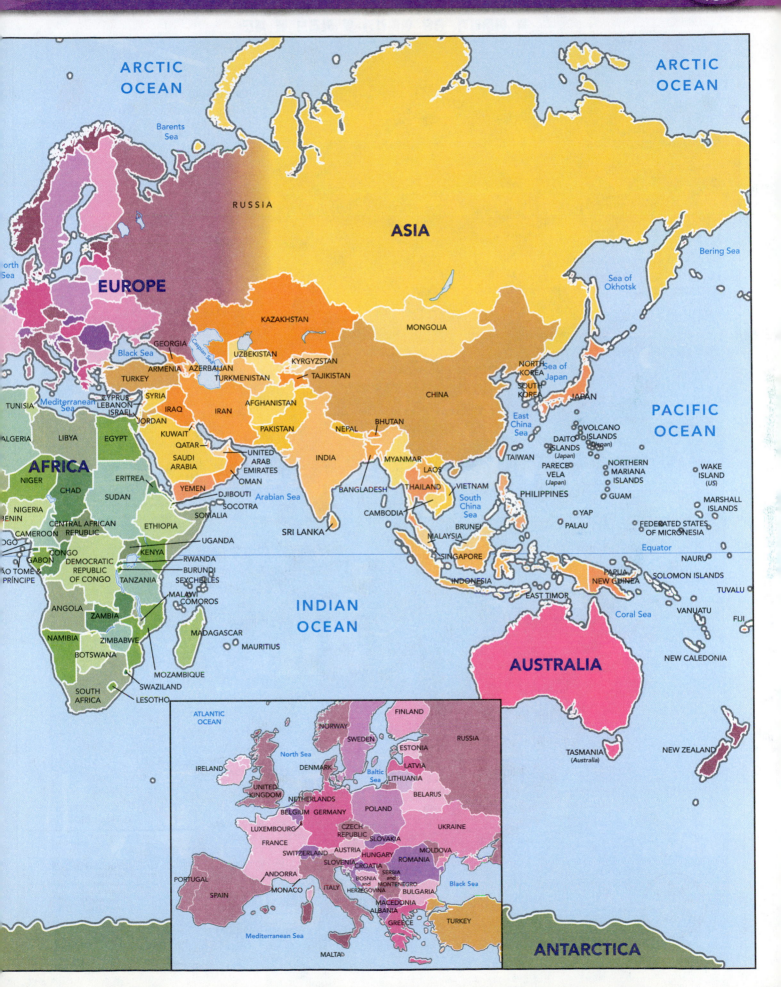

북 아메리카, 중앙 아메리카 및 카리브 해 제도

ARCTIC OCEAN

Bering Sea
Chukchi Sea
Bering Strait
Beaufort Sea

Greenland Sea
ICELAND
Reykjavik
Denmark Strait

Alaska
Gulf of Alaska

GREENLAND
Baffin Bay
Davis Strait
Nuuk (Godthab)

Yukon Territory
Northwest Territories
Nunavut
Hudson Strait
Ungava Bay
Labrador Sea

British Columbia
Alberta
Saskatchewan
Manitoba
CANADA
Hudson Bay
Newfoundland and Labrador

Washington
Montana
North Dakota
Minnesota
Ontario
Québec
Prince Edward Island
New Brunswick
Maine
Nova Scotia

Oregon
Idaho
Wyoming
South Dakota
Wisconsin
Michigan
Ottawa
New York
Vermont
New Hampshire
Massachusetts
Rhode Island
Connecticut
New Jersey
Delaware
Maryland

Nevada
California
Utah
Colorado
Nebraska
Iowa
UNITED STATES of AMERICA
Kansas
Missouri
Illinois
Indiana
Ohio
Pennsylvania
West Virginia
Virginia
Washington, DC

ATLANTIC OCEAN

Arizona
New Mexico
Oklahoma
Arkansas
Tennessee
Kentucky
North Carolina
South Carolina

Baja California
Sonora
Chihuahua
Coahuila
Texas
Louisiana
Mississippi
Alabama
Georgia
Florida

BERMUDA

Baja California Sur
Gulf of California
Durango
Nuevo León
Sinaloa
Zacatecas
Tamaulipas
Nayarit
MEXICO
San Luis Potosí
Querétaro
Hidalgo
Gulf of Mexico

Aguascalientes
Jalisco
Guanajuato
Colima
Michoacán
México
Morelos
Mexico City
Distrito Federal
Tlaxcala
Puebla
Veracruz
Guerrero
Oaxaca
Tabasco
Chiapas
Yucatán
Quintana Roo
Campeche

Nassau
THE BAHAMAS
Havana
CUBA
DOMINICAN REPUBLIC
HAITI
Port-au-Prince
Santo Domingo
PUERTO RICO
Kingston
JAMAICA

BELIZE
Belmopan
Gulf of Tehuantepec
GUATEMALA
HONDURAS
Guatemala City
Tegucigalpa
San Salvador
EL SALVADOR
NICARAGUA
Managua
San José
COSTA RICA
Panama City
PANAMA

Caribbean Sea

DOMINICAN REPUBLIC
Santo Domingo
PUERTO RICO
San Juan
VIRGIN ISLANDS
ANGUILLA
SAINT KITTS AND NEVIS
ANTIGUA AND BARBUDA
MONTSERRAT
GUADELOUPE
DOMINICA
MARTINIQUE
SAINT LUCIA
SAINT VINCENT AND THE GRENADINES
NETHERLANDS ANTILLES
ARUBA
BARBADOS
GRENADA
TRINIDAD AND TOBAGO

Caribbean Sea

PACIFIC OCEAN

N
W   E
S

0   500 Miles
0   500 KM

남 아메리카

Caribbean Sea

Barranquilla
Cartagena • • Maracaibo
Valencia
Barquisimeto • ★ Caracas
VENEZUELA

Medellín •
★ Bogotá
• Cali
COLOMBIA

Georgetown •
GUYANA
Paramaribo •
★ ★ Cayenne
SURINAME **FRENCH GUIANA**

ATLANTIC OCEAN

Equator
Quito ★
ECUADOR
Gulf of Guayaquil
• Guayaquil

Equator

• Belém
Manaus •
Fortaleza •
Teresina •
Recife •

PERU
★ Lima

BRAZIL

Salvador •

★ La Paz
BOLIVIA
Sucre •

Goiânia • ★ Brasília
Belo Horizonte •

PARAGUAY
CHILE
Asuncion ★

Rio de Janeiro •
Campinas •
São Paulo •
Curitiba •

PACIFIC OCEAN

Pôrto Alegre •

ARGENTINA
• Córdoba
Rosario •
Santiago ★
Buenos Aires ★
URUGUAY
Montevideo •

Gulf of San Matías

ATLANTIC OCEAN

Gulf of San Jorge

N
W ★ E
S

Strait of Magellan

FALKLAND ISLANDS
Port Stanley •

SOUTH GEORGIA ISLAND

0   500 Miles
0   500 KM

유럽

아프리카와 중동

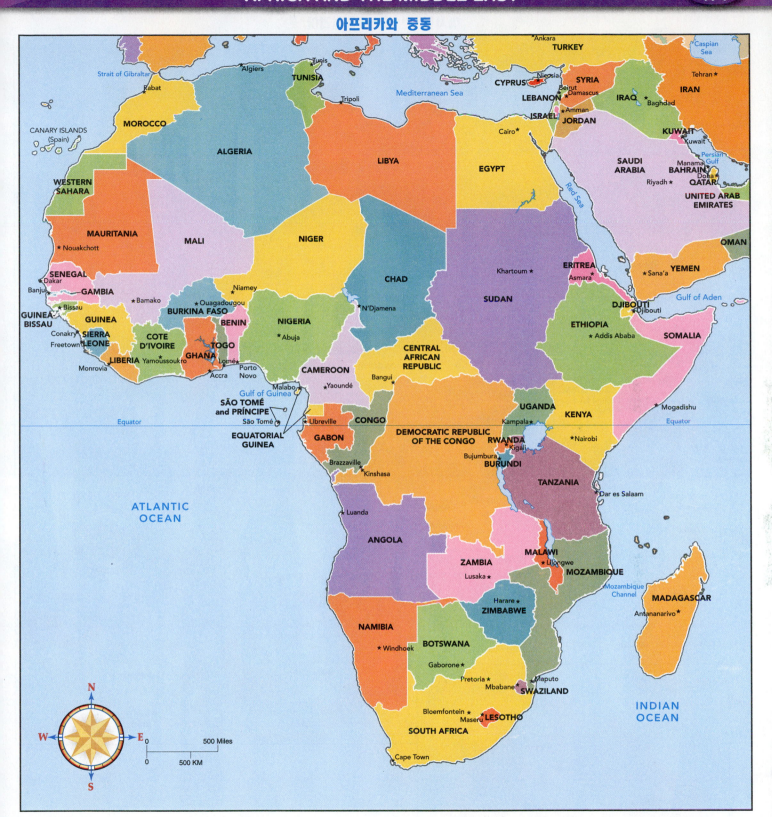

국가, 국적 및 언어

Country	Nationality	Language	Country	Nationality	Language
Afghanistan	Afghan	Afghan	Italy	Italian	Italian
Argentina	Argentine	Spanish	Japan	Japanese	Japanese
Australia	Australian	English	Jordan	Jordanian	Arabic
Bolivia	Bolivian	Spanish	Korea	Korean	Korean
Brazil	Brazilian	Portuguese	Laos	Laotian	Laotian
Bulgaria	Bulgarian	Bulgarian	Latvia	Latvian	Latvian
Cambodia	Cambodian	Cambodian	Lebanon	Lebanese	Arabic
Canada	Canadian	English/French	Lithuania	Lithuanian	Lithuanian
Chile	Chilean	Spanish	Malaysia	Malaysian	Malay
China	Chinese	Chinese	Mexico	Mexican	Spanish
Colombia	Colombian	Spanish	New Zealand	New Zealander	English
Costa Rica	Costa Rican	Spanish	Nicaragua	Nicaraguan	Spanish
Cuba	Cuban	Spanish	Norway	Norwegian	Norwegian
(The) Czech Republic	Czech	Czech	Pakistan	Pakistani	Urdu
Denmark	Danish	Danish	Panama	Panamanian	Spanish
(The) Dominican Republic	Dominican	Spanish	Peru	Peruvian	Spanish
Ecuador	Ecuadorian	Spanish	(The) Philippines	Filipino	Tagalog
Egypt	Egyptian	Arabic	Poland	Polish	Polish
El Salvador	Salvadorean	Spanish	Portugal	Portuguese	Portuguese
England	English	English	Puerto Rico	Puerto Rican	Spanish
Estonia	Estonian	Estonian	Romania	Romanian	Romanian
Ethiopia	Ethiopian	Amharic	Russia	Russian	Russian
Finland	Finnish	Finnish	Saudi Arabia	Saudi	Arabic
France	French	French	Slovakia	Slovak	Slovak
Germany	German	German	Spain	Spanish	Spanish
Greece	Greek	Greek	Sweden	Swedish	Swedish
Guatemala	Guatemalan	Spanish	Switzerland	Swiss	German/French/Italian
Haiti	Haitian	Haitian Kreyol	Taiwan	Taiwanese	Chinese
Honduras	Honduran	Spanish	Thailand	Thai	Thai
Hungary	Hungarian	Hungarian	Turkey	Turkish	Turkish
India	Indian	Hindi	Ukraine	Ukrainian	Ukrainian
Indonesia	Indonesian	Indonesian	(The) United States	American	English
Israel	Israeli	Hebrew	Venezuela	Venezuelan	Spanish
			Vietnam	Vietnamese	Vietnamese

A. Where are you from?
B. I'm from **Mexico**.

A. What's your nationality?
B. I'm **Mexican**.

A. What language do you speak?
B. I speak **Spanish**.

Tell about yourself: Where are you from? What's your nationality? What languages do you speak?

Now interview and tell about a friend.

동사 목록

규칙 동사

규칙 동사는 과거 및 과거 완료 시제일 경우 아래와 같이 4가지 형태로 철자가 변합니다.

1 동사의 끝에 **-ed**를 붙입니다. 보기:

act → act**ed**

act	cook	grill	pass	simmer
add	correct	guard	peel	sort
answer	cough	hand (in)	plant	spell
appear	cover	help	play	sprain
ask	crash	insert	polish	steam
assist	cross (out)	invent	pour	stow
attack	deliver	iron	print	stretch
attend	deposit	kick	reach	surf
bank	design	land	record	swallow
board	discuss	leak	register	talk
boil	dress	learn	relax	turn
box	drill	lengthen	repair	twist
brainstorm	dust	lift	repeat	unload
broil	edit	listen	request	vacuum
brush	end	load	respond	vomit
burn	enter	look	rest	walk
burp	establish	lower	return	wash
carpool	explain	mark	roast	watch
cash	faint	match	rock	wax
check	fasten	mix	saute	weed
clean	fix	mow	scratch	whiten
clear	floss	obey	seat	work
collect	fold	open	select	
comb	follow	paint	shorten	
construct	form	park	sign	

2 **-e**로 끝나는 동사에는 **-d**를 붙입니다. 보기:

assemble → assemble**d**

assemble	declare	grate	pronounce	shave
bake	describe	hire	prune	slice
balance	dislocate	manage	raise	sneeze
barbecue	dive	measure	rake	state
bathe	dribble	microwave	recite	style
bounce	enforce	move	recycle	supervise
browse	erase	nurse	remove	translate
bruise	examine	operate	revise	type
bubble	exchange	organize	rinse	underline
change	exercise	overdose	save	unscramble
circle	experience	practice	scrape	use
close	file	prepare	serve	vote
combine	gargle	produce	share	wheeze

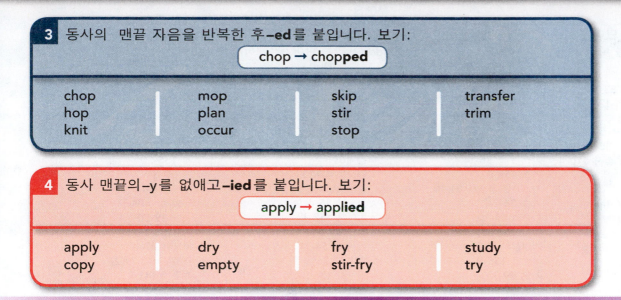

3 동사의 맨끝 자음을 반복한 후 **-ed**를 붙입니다. 보기:

chop → chop**ped**

chop	mop	skip	transfer
hop	plan	stir	trim
knit	occur	stop	

4 동사 맨끝의 **-y**를 없애고 **-ied**를 붙입니다. 보기:

apply → appl**ied**

| apply | dry | fry | study |
| copy | empty | stir-fry | try |

불규칙 동사

아래의 동사들은 불규칙 과거 및 과거분사 시제 형태를 가집니다.

be	was/were	been		know	knew	known
beat	beat	beaten		leave	left	left
become	became	become		let	let	let
bend	bent	bent		make	made	made
begin	began	begun		meet	met	met
bleed	bled	bled		pay	paid	paid
break	broke	broken		put	put	put
bring	brought	brought		read	read	read
build	built	built		rewrite	rewrote	rewritten
buy	bought	bought		run	ran	run
catch	caught	caught		ring	rang	rung
choose	chose	chosen		say	said	said
come	came	come		see	saw	seen
cut	cut	cut		sell	sold	sold
do	did	done		set	set	set
draw	drew	drawn		shoot	shot	shot
drink	drank	drunk		sing	sang	sung
drive	drove	driven		sit	sat	sat
eat	ate	eaten		sleep	slept	slept
fall	fell	fallen		speak	spoke	spoken
feed	fed	fed		stand	stood	stood
fly	flew	flown		sweep	swept	swept
get	got	gotten		swim	swam	swum
give	gave	given		swing	swung	swung
go	went	gone		take	took	taken
grow	grew	grown		teach	taught	taught
hang	hung	hung		throw	threw	thrown
have	had	had		understand	understood	understood
hit	hit	hit		withdraw	withdrew	withdrawn
hold	held	held		write	wrote	written
hurt	hurt	hurt				

용어집

고딕체 숫자는 그 단어가 실린 페이지를 나타냅니다. 그 다음에 나오는 숫자는 삽화에서의 위치와 그 페이지에 실린 단어 리스트에서의 위치를 나타냅니다. 예를 들면, "address 1-5"는 address라는 단어가 1페이지에 있으며, 아이템 번호는 5번이라는 뜻입니다.

용어집

고딕체 숫자는 그 단어가 실린 페이지를 나타냅니다. 그 다음에 나오는 숫자는 삽화에서의 위치와 그 페이지에 실린 단어 리스트에서의 위치를 나타냅니다. 예를 들면, "address 1-5"는 address라는 단어가 1페이지에 있으며, 아이템 번호는 5번이라는 뜻입니다.

숫자, 요일, 월

Cardinal Numbers

1	one
2	two
3	three
4	four
5	five
6	six
7	seven
8	eight
9	nine
10	ten
11	eleven
12	twelve
13	thirteen
14	fourteen
15	fifteen
16	sixteen
17	seventeen
18	eighteen
19	nineteen
20	twenty
21	twenty-one
22	twenty-two
30	thirty
40	forty
50	fifty
60	sixty
70	seventy
80	eighty
90	ninety
100	one hundred
101	one hundred (and) one
102	one hundred (and) two
1,000	one thousand
10,000	ten thousand
100,000	one hundred thousand
1,000,000	one million
1,000,000,000	one billion

Ordinal Numbers

1st	first
2nd	second
3rd	third
4th	fourth
5th	fifth
6th	sixth
7th	seventh
8th	eighth
9th	ninth
10th	tenth
11th	eleventh
12th	twelfth
13th	thirteenth
14th	fourteenth
15th	fifteenth
16th	sixteenth
17th	seventeenth
18th	eighteenth
19th	nineteenth
20th	twentieth
21st	twenty-first
22nd	twenty-second
30th	thirtieth
40th	fortieth
50th	fiftieth
60th	sixtieth
70th	seventieth
80th	eightieth
90th	ninetieth
100th	one hundredth
101st	one hundred (and) first
102nd	one hundred (and) second
1,000th	one thousandth
10,000th	ten thousandth
100,000th	one hundred thousandth
1,000,000th	one millionth
1,000,000,000th	one billionth

Days of the Week

Sunday
Monday
Tuesday
Wednesday
Thursday
Friday
Saturday

Months of the Year

January	July
February	August
March	September
April	October
May	November
June	December

주제별 색인